UNDERSTANDING
CULTURAL
DIFFERENCES

UNDERSTANDING CULTURAL DIFFERENCES

Edward T. Hall and Mildred Reed Hall

INTERCULTURAL PRESS, INC.

For information, contact:
Intercultural Press, Inc.
P.O. Box 700
Yarmouth, Maine 04096

Printed in the United States of America

99 98 97 96 95 94   8 9 10 11 12 13

First published in hardcover, 1990.

Library of Congress Cataloging-in-Publication Data

Hall, Edward Twitchell, 1914-
 Understanding cultural differences: keys to success in West Germany, France, and the United States/Edward T. Hall, Mildred Reed Hall.
 p.cm.
 Includes bibliographical references.
 ISBN 0-933662-84-X (hardcover)
 ISBN 1-877864-07-2 (paperback)
 1. Industrial management—Cross-cultural studies. 2. Industrial management—United States. 3. Industrial management—France. 4. Industrial management—Germany (West) 5. Corporations, American-France—Management. 6. Corporations, American—Management. 7. National characteristics, American. 8. National characteristics, French. 9. National characteristics, West German. I. Hall, Mildred Reed. II. Title.

HD31.H229   1989   89-84388
306-dc20

This book is dedicated with gratitude and appreciation to all the people at *Stern*/Gruner & Jahr who provided unfailing support and encouragement throughout our work together and to the many people we interviewed in West Germany, France, and the United States who freely shared their experiences with us and helped us understand the complex interactions between the peoples of these different cultures.

Contents

Contents

CONTENTS

Preface

This book is designed to help American businesspeople understand German and French psychology and behavior and to show how Americans perceive the Germans and the French. However, to understand others, we must also understand ourselves; thus, the last section on the United States presents a brief analysis of the psychology and behavior of Americans. It is our hope that this section will in addition prove helpful to German and French readers who are just as baffled by American behavior as Americans are by theirs. Our main emphasis is not on economics, politics, or history, but on the subtle yet powerful impact of culturally conditioned behavior on the conduct of international business.

Often Germans seem stiff and pompous to Americans while Americans seem sloppy and superficial to Germans. The French think Americans are enthusiastic but lacking in style; Americans feel the French take forever to get down to business. Germans think the French are not serious enough; the French think the Germans lack sophistication.

In fact, each country simply has its own way of seeing and doing things, based on unstated rules, and these hidden differences often make cooperation difficult. This book is an attempt to help break the logjam caused by culturally based misunderstandings.

Even though culture is experienced personally, it is nonetheless a shared system. A Frenchman enjoys the extravagance of rhetorical flourish, and other French people do not find this foolish—although a German probably would. Because culture is experienced personally, very few individuals see it for what it is—*a program for behavior*. Members of a common culture not only share information, they share methods of coding, storing and retrieving that information. These methods vary from culture to culture. Knowing what kind of information people from other cultures require is one key to effective international communication.

Viewed from the outside, each culture has "hidden codes" of behavior, which can rarely be understood without a "code breaker." Communications experts estimate that 90 percent or more of all communication is conveyed by means other than language, in a culture's *nonverbal* messages. These messages are taken for granted and transmitted more or less unconsciously. For example, American culture requires that people smile and greet one another when they arrive at work in the morning; such behavior is automatic. In Mexico and other Latin American countries people not only smile and greet coworkers but also shake hands and exchange a few words about family or other personal matters. If these gestures are omitted, everyone in the office will assume something is wrong or will be offended. Nonverbal messages are highly situational in character; they apply to specific situations and are seldom explained in words. The meanings of such messages are unique to each culture and often charged with emotion.

This book is divided into four parts. Part 1, "Key Concepts," describes conceptual frames or special lenses designed to bring into focus foreign patterns of thought and behavior—conceptual hooks on which to hang ideas and observations. For example, in some cultures it is respectful to avoid direct eye contact while in other cultures that same behavior is considered evasive or even hostile. Why? Part 1 introduces the reader to the larger underlying systems of behavior that endow such simple actions with special significance, and it provides the foundation or the context for behavior.

The next three sections, parts 2, 3, and 4, describe the basic patterns that characterize the Germans, the French and the

Americans. The focus is on the specific differences among these three cultures in the way business is conducted. To take a brief example, if a subordinate performs poorly in the United States, a good American manager will find something to praise before criticizing the worker. A good German manager will address the problem directly; praise coupled with criticism only confuses German employees. In France a good manager will find a subtle way of conveying displeasure, perhaps by removal of part of a support system. Despite these different approaches, each message will come across loud and clear to each recipient, who is programmed to the particular culture. In these sections, we discuss a wide variety of topics, including dealing with hierarchies, styles of decision making, rules for negotiating, and the handling of time and space.

The life patterns of a complex civilization cannot be covered fully in a single book, yet it is possible to describe some of the principal contrasting patterns. The specific examples provided in parts 2, 3, and 4 must be considered as illustrative of larger basic patterns rather than as isolated fragments or mere generalizations.

Resist the temptation to plunge immediately into part 2, that is, to skip the conceptual introduction and go directly to the sections on the specific cultures. The ultimate usefulness of this book will be greater if its contents are digested in sequence, using part 1 as a foundation for what follows.

In writing this book we were especially mindful of the duties and responsibilities of chief executive officers and company directors. In today's business world, they, more than anyone else, are responsible for their companies' performance and economic health. Informed CEOs are a crucial element in the early, critical phases of a company's foreign operations. Unless top management pays attention to the messages of this book, no one else will; a gram of insight at the top is worth a kilo at the lower levels.

To quote one experienced vice president for international operations of a large firm, commenting on the responsibilities of top management: "Foreign operations are my most difficult assignment, day in and day out. However, they may hold even greater long-range potential for sales and profit than our domestic business."

Although this book was written primarily for businesspeople, because it is oriented toward interpersonal relations with foreigners it is useful for many other people whose lives involve contact with foreign nationals, either in their personal or professional lives: officials in government or private foundations, teachers who have students from other cultures, educators working abroad or at home with various ethnic groups, and ordinary people whose lives and work bring them in contact with those whose national or ethnic backgrounds are different from their own (not to mention those who are married to foreigners).

For the past thirty years we have conducted research in the field of intercultural communication: designing programs for the selection and training of people working in foreign cultures, consulting to international business, and writing books and articles on the intercultural process. We specialize in identifying the nonverbal components of intercultural communication— the unspoken signals and assumptions that flow from human psychology and national character, elements crucial to success in business.

As part of our research for this book, we conducted 180 interviews in the United States, West Germany, and France. We were most fortunate to have had the assistance of a wide range of exceptionally talented and knowledgeable women and men with years of "hands-on" experience in business. Their knowledge and experience helped shape our work; we are indeed grateful for their cooperation, honesty, and generosity.

Acknowledgments

This book is an outgrowth of a project we completed for the German publisher Gruner & Jahr. One of their publications, *Stern,* originally approached us to write handbooks for German business. *Stern*/Gruner & Jahr deserve special recognition for sponsoring our work and publishing three sets of books on cultural differences in business, which they distributed as a public service in Europe and the United States. We wish to acknowledge *Stern*'s active cooperation and unfailing support for our work. In particular we thank Herrn Rolf Grimm, M. Edmond Jacquemot, Herrn Lothar Neffe, Frau Julie Penzel, and Herrn John Ritchhart.

We are very grateful to Judith Appelbaum and Florence Janovic of Sensible Solutions, Inc., for their unflagging support and encouragement and their practical advice and assistance with this book for American readers. We thank Sally Arteseros for her advice on the manuscript and we acknowledge with thanks the suggestions of David Hoopes of the Intercultural Press.

We wish to express particular appreciation to Judy Karasik for her skillful editing and to Jana Oyler for her excellent suggestions, her helpful editing, and her untiring performance on the word processor through many revisions.

Edward T. Hall and Mildred Reed Hall

Introduction

Until now there has been no way to translate behavior from one culture to another. While there are many good books on foreign cultures, most of them present bits and pieces of information; others contain theories about social, economic, or political organization. Few books provide readers with a framework for integrating their own observations and experiences.

With this book we hope to provide the reader with such a framework by revealing the underlying patterns of behavior. These patterns show the critical relationships between different parts of the culture, and they integrate what were formerly thought of as isolated fragments.

Because cultures are unified entities in which everything interrelates, it is of critical importance when studying them to pay attention to data from a broad range of sources: novels, newspapers, magazines, film, and TV; the structure and behavior of business and civic institutions; the behavior of individuals and groups.

In preparing this study, we conducted in-depth, open-ended interviews with a carefully selected sample of individuals from business and the professions. We also interviewed writers, artists, and educators. Our firsthand observations and these lengthy interviews, coupled with sophisticated models of culture, have enabled us to identify some of the major cultural patterns that business executives need to keep in mind when dealing with their counterparts in other countries.

Of course there are individual differences—including ethnic differences—within every country. This is particularly true of countries such as the United States, West Germany, and France, whose many regions have various minicultures of their own. In this study, when we refer to "French behavior," we refer to the French businesspeople working in large metropolitan areas such as Paris and Lyon. When we refer to Germans, we mean business executives in the industrialized centers of West Germany: Frankfurt, Düsseldorf, Köln, Hamburg, etc.

Scientists in the intercultural field are vulnerable to distortions from two directions. First, they are subject to the implicit perceptions of their own culture. Whether willingly or unconsciously, they look at any new culture through eyes conditioned from birth to see things in a particular way. Second, scientists are frequently taught theories, assumptions, and hypotheses that may create barriers between the observer and the culture being studied.

As scientists and observers of microcultural differences, we guard constantly against these two forms of distortion. The implicit perception of our own culture is more difficult to surmount than theories and assumptions; years of experience have made us sensitive to the danger signs of both. Each time we approach a new culture, we cannot predict what we will find or how the parts of the cultural puzzle will ultimately fit together. We know, for example, that for each culture communication can be placed somewhere on the scale of high- to low-context, but we don't know where it fits until actual communication patterns have been analyzed. We search for specific examples of basic patterns: where individuals of a given culture can be placed on various scales; how information flows (freely or through restricted channels); whether power is centralized or diffused; how decisions are made and by whom; how people conduct interpersonal relationships; how much close personal contact and confidence exist between people, etc. The key concepts delineated in part 1 of this book are provided as structures to help the reader integrate the major cultural patterns she or he will encounter.

We have no particular theoretical, ideological, or political bias. Our objective is to make a contribution to international understanding and to help reduce tensions that result from the many different "silent languages" people use. This book's goal is to maximize success for American executives conducting business with the Germans and the French and to identify some of the hidden obstacles on which numerous companies have already foundered.

PART 1

Key Concepts: Underlying Structures of Culture

CULTURE IS COMMUNICATION

In physics today, so far as we know, the galaxies that one studies are all controlled by the same laws. This is not entirely true of the worlds created by humans. Each cultural world operates according to its own internal dynamic, its own principles, and its own laws—written and unwritten. Even time and space are unique to each culture. There are, however, some common threads that run through all cultures.

It is possible to say that the world of communication can be divided into three parts: *words, material things,* and *behavior.* Words are the medium of business, politics, and diplomacy. Material things are usually indicators of status and power. Behavior provides feedback on how other people feel and includes techniques for avoiding confrontation.

By studying these three parts of the communication process in our own and other cultures, we can come to recognize and understand a vast unexplored region of human behavior that exists outside the range of people's conscious awareness, a "silent language" that is usually conveyed unconsciously (see Edward T. Hall's *The Silent Language*). This silent language includes a broad range of evolutionary concepts, practices, and solutions to problems which have their roots not in the lofty ideas of philosophers but in the shared experiences of ordinary people. In the words of the director of a project on cross-cultural relations, understanding the silent language "provides insights into *the underlying principles that shape our lives."* These underlying principles are not only inherently interesting but eminently practical. The readers of this book, whether they be German, French, American, or from other countries, should find these principles useful at home and abroad.

Culture can be likened to a giant, extraordinary complex, subtle computer. Its programs guide the actions and responses of human beings in every walk of life. This process requires attention to everything people do to survive, advance in the world, and gain satisfaction from life. Furthermore, cultural programs will not work if crucial steps are omitted, which happens when people unconsciously apply their own rules to another system.

During the three years we worked on this book, we had to learn two different programs for our office computer. The first was quite simple, but mastery did require paying close attention to every detail and several weeks of practice. The second was a much more complex program that required weeks of intensive practice, hours of tutoring, and days of depression and frustration when "the darn thing didn't work." Learning a new cultural program is infinitely more complicated and requires years of practice, yet there are many similarities in the learning process.

Cultural communications are deeper and more complex than spoken or written messages. *The essence of effective cross-cultural communication has more to do with releasing the right responses than with sending the "right" messages.* We offer here some conceptual tools to help our readers decipher the complex, unspoken rules of each culture.

FAST AND SLOW MESSAGES: FINDING THE APPROPRIATE SPEED

The speed with which a particular message can be decoded and acted on is an important characteristic of human communication. There are fast and slow messages. A headline or cartoon, for example, is fast; the meaning that one extracts from books or art is slow. A fast message sent to people who are geared to a slow format will usually miss the target. While the content of the wrong-speed message may be understandable, it won't be received by someone accustomed to or expecting a different speed. The problem is that few people are aware that information can be sent at different speeds.

4

EXAMPLES OF FAST AND SLOW MESSAGES

Fast Messages	Slow Messages
Prose	Poetry
Headlines	Books
A communique	An ambassador
Propaganda	Art
Cartoons	Etchings
TV commercials	TV documentary
Television	Print
Easy familiarity	Deep relationships
Manners	Culture

Almost everything in life can be placed somewhere along the fast/slow message-speed spectrum. Such things as diplomacy, research, writing books, and creating art are accomplished in the slow mode. Buddha, Confucius, Shakespeare, Goethe, and Rembrandt all produced messages that human beings are still deciphering hundreds of years after the fact. Language is a very slow message; after 4,000 years, human beings are just beginning to discover what language is all about. The same can be said of culture, which incorporates multiple styles of "languages" that only release messages to those who are willing to spend the time to understand them.

In essence a person is a slow message; it takes time to get to know someone well. The message is, of course, slower in some cultures than in others. In the United States it is not too difficult to get to know people quickly in a relatively superficial way, which is all that most Americans want. Foreigners have often commented on how "unbelievably friendly" the Americans are. However, when Edward T. Hall studied the subject for the U.S. State Department, he discovered a worldwide complaint about Americans: they seem capable of forming only one kind of friendship—the informal, superficial kind that does not involve an exchange of deep confidences.

Conversely, in Europe personal relationships and friendships are highly valued and tend to take a long time to solidify. This is largely a function of the long-lasting, well-established networks of friends and relationships—particularly among the French—that one finds in Europe. Although there are exceptions, as a rule it will take Americans longer than they expect to really get to know Europeans. It is difficult, and at times may even be impossible, for a foreigner to break into these networks. Nevertheless, many businesspeople have found it expedient to take the time and make the effort to develop genuine friends among their business associates.

HIGH AND LOW CONTEXT: HOW MUCH INFORMATION IS ENOUGH?

Context is the information that surrounds an event; it is inextricably bound up with the meaning of that event. The elements that combine to produce a given meaning—events and context—are in different proportions depending on the culture. The cultures of the world can be compared on a scale from high to low context.

A high context (HC) communication or message is one in which *most* of the information is already in the person, while very little is in the coded, explicit, transmitted part of the message. A low context (LC) communication is just the opposite; i.e., the mass of the information is vested in the explicit code. Twins who have grown up together can and do communicate more economically (HC) than two lawyers in a courtroom during a trial (LC), a mathematician programming a computer, two politicians drafting legislation, two administrators writing a regulation.

Edward T. Hall, 1976

Japanese, Arabs, and Mediterranean peoples, who have extensive information networks among family, friends, colleagues, and clients and who are involved in close personal relationships, are high-context. As a result, for most normal transactions in daily life they do not require, nor do they expect, much in-depth, background information. This is because they keep

6

themselves informed about everything having to do with the people who are important in their lives. Low-context people include Americans, Germans, Swiss, Scandinavians, and other northern Europeans; they compartmentalize their personal relationships, their work, and many aspects of day-to-day life. Consequently, each time they interact with others they need detailed background information. The French are much higher on the context scale than either the Germans or the Americans. This difference can affect virtually every situation and every relationship in which the members of these two opposite traditions find themselves.

Within each culture, of course, there are specific individual differences in the need for contexting—the process of filling in background data. But it is helpful to know whether the culture of a particular country falls on the high or low side of the scale since every person is influenced by the level of context.

Contexting performs multiple functions. For example, any shift in the level of context is a communication. The shift can be up the scale, indicating a warming of the relationship, or down the scale (lowering the context), communicating coolness or displeasure—signaling something has gone wrong with a relationship. In the United States the boss might communicate annoyance to an assistant when he shifts from the high-context, familiar form of address to the low-context, formal form of address. When this happens the boss is telling the subordinate in no uncertain terms that she or he has stepped out of line and incurred disfavor. In Japan moving the direction of the context is a source of daily feedback as to how things are going. The day starts with the use of honorifics, formal forms of address attached to each name. If things are going well the honorifics are dropped as the day progresses. First-naming in the United States is an artificial attempt at high-contexting; it tends to offend Europeans, who view the use of first names as acceptable only between close friends and family. With Europeans, one is always safe using a formal form of address, waiting for the other person to indicate when familiarity is acceptable.

7

Like their near relations the Germans, many Anglo-Americans (mostly those of northern European heritage) are not only low-context but they also lack extensive, well-developed information networks. American networks are limited in scope and development compared to those of the French, the Spanish, the Italians, and the Japanese. What follows from this is that Americans, unless they are very unsophisticated, will feel the need for contexting, for detailed background information, any time they are asked to make a decision or to do something. The American approach to life is quite segmented and focused on discrete, compartmentalized information; Americans need to know what is going to be in what compartment before they commit themselves. We experienced this in Japan when we were asked on short notice to provide names of well-placed Japanese and Americans to be participants in a small conference. Like most prudent Americans, we were reluctant to provide names until we knew what the conference was about and what the individuals recommended would be expected to do. This seemed logical and reasonable enough to us. Nevertheless, our reluctance was read as obstructionist by our Japanese colleagues and friends responsible for the conference. In Japan the mere presence of certain individuals endows the group and its activities with authority and status, which is far more important than the topic of the conference. It is characteristic of high-context, high-information societies that attendance at functions is as much a matter of the prestige associated with the function as anything else. This in turn means that, quite frequently, invitations to high-level meetings and conferences will be issued on short notice. It is taken for granted that those invited will eschew all previous commitments if the meeting is important enough. As a general rule Americans place greater importance on how long ago a commitment was made, on the agenda, and on the relevance of the expertise of different individuals to the agenda. (For an in-depth discussion of the Japanese, we refer the reader to the authors' *Hidden Differences: Doing Business with the Japanese,* in the reading list.)

Another example of the contrast between how high- and low-context systems work is this: consider a top American executive working in an office and receiving a normal quota of visitors, usually one at a time. Most of the information that is relevant to the job originates from the few people the executive sees in the course of the day, as well as from what she or he reads. This is why the advisors and support personnel who surround the presidents of American enterprises (as well as the president of the United States) are so important. They and they alone control the content and the flow of organizational information to the chief executive.

Contrast this with the office of virtually any business executive in a high-context country such as France or Japan, where information flows freely and from all sides. Not only are people constantly coming and going, both seeking and giving information, but the entire form and function of the organization is centered on gathering, processing, and disseminating information. Everyone stays informed about every aspect of the business and knows who is best informed on what subjects.

In Germany almost everything is low-context and compartmentalized. The executive office is both a refuge and a screen— a refuge for the boss from the distractions of day-to-day office interactions and a screen for the employees from continual supervision. Information communicated in the office is not shared except with a select few—the exact antithesis of the high-information cultures.

High-context people are apt to become impatient and irritated when low-context people insist on giving them information they don't need. Conversely, low-context people are at a loss when high-context people do not provide *enough* information. One of the great communications challenges in life is to find the appropriate level of contexting needed in each situation. Too much information leads people to feel they are being talked down to; too little information can mystify them or make them feel left out. Ordinarily, people make these adjustments automatically in their own country, but in other countries their messages frequently miss the target.

The other side of the coin when considering context level is the apparent paradox that high-context people, such as the French, want to see *everything* when evaluating a *new* enterprise to which they have not been contexted. Annual reports or tax returns are not enough. Furthermore, they will keep asking until they get the information they want. Being high context, the French are driven to make their own synthesis of the meanings of the figures. Unlike Americans, they feel uncomfortable with someone else's synthesis, someone else's "bottom line."

SPACE

Every living thing has a visible physical boundary—its skin—separating it from its external environment. This visible boundary is surrounded by a series of invisible boundaries that are more difficult to define but are just as real. These other boundaries begin with the individual's personal space and terminate with her or his "territory."

Territoriality

Territoriality, an innate characteristic whose roots lie hundreds of millions of years in the past, is the act of laying claim to and defending a territory and is a vital link in the chain of events necessary for survival. In humans territoriality is highly developed and strongly influenced by culture. It is particularly well developed in the Germans and the Americans. Americans tend to establish places that they label "mine"—a cook's feeling about a kitchen or a child's view of her or his bedroom. In Germany this same feeling of territoriality is commonly extended to all possessions, including the automobile. If a German's car is touched, it is as though the individual himself has been touched.

Space also communicates power. A corner office suite in the United States is conventionally occupied by "the brass," and a private office in any location has more status than a desk in the

10

open without walls. In both German and American business, the top floors are reserved for high-ranking officials and executives. In contrast, important French officials occupy a position in the *middle*, surrounded by subordinates; the emphasis there is on occupying the central position in an information network, where one can stay informed and can control what is happening.

Personal Space

Personal space is another form of territory. Each person has around him an invisible bubble of space which expands and contracts depending on a number of things: the relationship to the people nearby, the person's emotional state, cultural background, and the activity being performed. Few people are allowed to penetrate this bit of mobile territory and then only for short periods of time. Changes in the bubble brought about by cramped quarters or crowding cause people to feel uncomfortable or aggressive. In northern Europe, the bubbles are quite large and people keep their distance. In southern France, Italy, Greece, and Spain, the bubbles get smaller and smaller so that the distance that is perceived as intimate in the north overlaps normal conversational distance in the south, all of which means that Mediterranean Europeans "get too close" to the Germans, the Scandinavians, the English, and those Americans of northern European ancestry. In northern Europe one does not touch others. Even the brushing of the overcoat sleeve used to elicit an apology.

The Multisensory Spatial Experience

Few people realize that space is perceived by *all* the senses, not by vision alone. Auditory space is perceived by the ears, thermal space by the skin, kinesthetic space by the muscles, and olfactory space by the nose. As one might imagine, there are great cultural differences in the programming of the senses. Americans to some extent and Germans to a greater extent rely heavily on auditory screening, particularly when they want to concentrate. High-context people reject auditory screening and thrive on being open to interruptions and in tune with what goes on around them. Hence, in French and Italian cities one is periodically and intrusively bombarded by noise.

Unconscious Reactions to Spatial Differences

Spatial changes give tone to communication, accent it, and at times even override the spoken word. As people interact, the flow and shift of distance between them is integral to the communication process. For example, if a stranger does not maintain "normal" conversational distance and gets too close, our reaction is automatic—we feel uncomfortable, sometimes even offended or threatened and we back up.

Human beings in the course of a lifetime incorporate literally hundreds of spatial cues. They imbibe the significance of these cues like mother's milk, in the context of their own culture. Just as a fragrance will trigger a memory, these cues and their associated behaviors release unconscious responses, regulating the tone, tempo, and mood of human transactions.

Since most people don't think about personal distance as something that is culturally patterned, foreign spatial cues are almost inevitably misinterpreted. This can lead to bad feelings which are then projected onto the people from the other culture in a most personal way. When a foreigner appears aggressive and pushy, or remote and cold, it may mean only that her or his personal distance is different from yours.

Americans have strong feelings about proximity and the attendant rights, responsibilities, and obligations associated with being a neighbor. Neighbors should be friendly and agreeable, cut their lawns, keep their places up, and do their bit for the neighborhood. By contrast, in France and Germany, simply sharing adjacent houses does not necessarily mean that people will interact with each other, particularly if they have not met socially. Proximity requires different behavior in other cultures.

12

TIME

Life on earth evolved in response to the cycles of day and night and the ebb and flow of the tides. As humans evolved, a multiplicity of internal biological clocks also developed. These biological clocks now regulate most of the physiological functions of our bodies. It is not surprising, therefore, that human concepts of time grew out of the natural rhythms associated with daily, monthly, and annual cycles. From the beginning humans have been tied to growing seasons and were dependent on the forces and rhythms of nature.

Out of this background two time systems evolved—one as an expression of our biological clocks, the other of the solar, lunar, and annual cycles. These systems will be described under the headings "Time As Structure" and "Time as Communication." In the sections that follow we restrict ourselves to those manifestations of time that have proved to be stumbling blocks at the cultural interface.

Monochronic and Polychronic Time

There are many kinds of time systems in the world, but two are most important to international business. We call them mono chronic and polychronic time. Monochronic time means paying attention to and doing only one thing at a time. Polychronic time means being involved with many things at once. Like oil and water, the two systems do not mix.

In monochronic cultures, time is experienced and used in a linear way—comparable to a road extending from the past into the future. Monochronic time is divided quite naturally into segments; it is scheduled and compartmentalized, making it possible for a person to concentrate on one thing at a time. In a monochronic system, the schedule may take priority above all else and be treated as sacred and unalterable.

Monochronic time is perceived as being almost *tangible:* people talk about it as though it were money, as something that can be "spent," "saved," "wasted," and "lost." It is also used as

13

a classification system for ordering life and setting priorities: "I don't have time to see him." Because monochronic time concentrates on one thing at a time, people who are governed by it don't like to be interrupted. Monochronic time seals people off from one another and, as a result, intensifies some relationships while shortchanging others. Time becomes a room which some people are allowed to enter, while others are excluded.

Monochronic time dominates most business in the United States. While Americans perceive it as almost in the air they breathe, it is nevertheless a learned product of northern European culture and is therefore arbitrary and imposed. Monochronic time is an artifact of the industrial revolution in England; factory life required the labor force to be on hand and in place at an appointed hour. In spite of the fact that it is *learned*, monochronic time now appears to be natural and logical because the great majority of Americans grew up in monochronic time systems with whistles and bells counting off the hours.

Other Western cultures—Switzerland, Germany, and Scandinavia in particular—are dominated by the iron hand of monochronic time as well. German and Swiss cultures represent classic examples of monochronic time. Still, monochronic time is not natural time; in fact, it seems to violate many of humanity's innate rhythms.

In almost every respect, polychronic systems are the antithesis of monochronic systems. Polychronic time is characterized by the simultaneous occurrence of many things and by a *great involvement with people.* There is more emphasis on completing human transactions than on holding to schedules. For example, two polychronic Latins conversing on a street corner would likely opt to be late for their next appointment rather than abruptly terminate the conversation before its natural conclusion. Polychronic time is experienced as much less tangible than monochronic time and can better be compared to a single point than to a road.

Proper understanding of the difference between the monochronic and polychronic time systems will be helpful in dealing with the time-flexible Mediterranean peoples. While the generalizations listed below do not apply equally to all cultures, they will help convey a pattern:

MONOCHRONIC PEOPLE	POLYCHRONIC PEOPLE
do one thing at a time	do many things at once
concentrate on the job	are highly distractible and subject to interruptions
take time commitments (deadlines, schedules) seriously	consider time commitments an objective to be achieved, if possible
are low-context and need information	are high-context and already have information
are committed to the job	are committed to people and human relationships
adhere religiously to plans	change plans often and easily
are concerned about not disturbing others; follow rules of privacy and consideration	are more concerned with those who are closely related (family, friends, close business associates) than with privacy
show great respect for private property; seldom borrow or lend	borrow and lend things often and easily
emphasize promptness	base promptness on the relationship
are accustomed to short-term relationships	have strong tendency to build lifetime relationships

The Relation between Time and Space

In monochronic time cultures the emphasis is on the compartmentalization of functions and people. Private offices are soundproof if possible. In polychronic Mediterranean cultures, business

15

offices often have large reception areas where people can wait. Company or government officials may even transact their business by moving about in the reception area, stopping to confer with this group and that one until everyone has been attended to.

Polychronic people feel that private space disrupts the flow of information by shutting people off from one another. In polychronic systems, appointments mean very little and may be shifted around even at the last minute to accommodate someone more important in an individual's hierarchy of family, friends, or associates. Some polychronic people (such as Latin Americans and Arabs) give precedence to their large circle of family members over any business obligation. Polychronic people also have many close friends and good clients with whom they spend a great deal of time. The close links to clients or customers creates a reciprocal feeling of obligation and a mutual desire to be helpful.

Polychronic Time and Information

Polychronic people live in a sea of information. They feel they must be up to the minute about everything and everybody, be it business or personal, and they seldom subordinate personal relationships to the exigencies of schedules or budgets.

It is impossible to know how many millions of dollars have been lost in international business because monochronic and polychronic people do not understand each other or even realize that two such different time systems exist. The following example illustrates how difficult it is for these two types to relate:

A French salesman working for a French company that had recently been bought by Americans found himself with a new American manager who expected instant results and higher profits immediately. Because of the emphasis on personal relationships, it frequently takes years to develop customers in polychronic France, and, in family-owned firms, relationships with customers

16

may span generations. The American manager, not understanding this, ordered the salesman to develop new customers within three months. The salesman knew this was impossible and had to resign, asserting his legal right to take with him all the loyal customers he had developed over the years. Neither side understood what had happened.

These two opposing views of time and personal relationships often show up during business meetings. In French meetings the information flow is high, and one is expected to read other people's thoughts, intuit the state of their business, and even garner indirectly what government regulations are in the offing. For the French and other polychronic/high-context people, a tight, fixed agenda can be an encumbrance, even an insult to one's intelligence. Most, if not all, of those present have a pretty good idea of what will be discussed beforehand. The purpose of the meeting is to create consensus. A rigid agenda and consensus represent opposite goals and do not mix. *The importance of this basic dichotomy cannot be overemphasized.*

Past- and Future-Oriented Countries

It is always important to know which segments of the time frame are emphasized. Cultures in countries such as Iran, India, and those of the Far East are past-oriented. Others, such as that of the urban United States, are oriented to the present and short-term future; still others, such as those of Latin America, are both past- and present-oriented. In Germany, where historical background is very important, every talk, book, or article begins with background information giving an historical perspective. This irritates many foreigners who keep wondering, "Why don't they get on with it? After all, I am educated. Don't the Germans know that?" The Japanese and the French are also steeped in history, but because they are high-context cultures, historical facts are alluded to obliquely. At present, there is no satisfactory explanation for why and how differences of this sort came about.

17

TIME AS COMMUNICATION

As surely as each culture has its spoken language, each has its own *language of time;* to function effectively in France, Germany, and the United States, it is essential to acquaint oneself with the local language of time. When we take our own time system for granted and project it onto other cultures, we fail to read the hidden messages in the foreign time system and thereby deny ourselves vital feedback.

For Americans, the use of appointment-schedule time reveals how people feel about each other, how significant their business is, and where they rank in the status system. Treatment of time can also convey a powerful form of insult. Furthermore, because the rules are informal, they operate largely out-of-awareness and, as a consequence, are less subject to conscious manipulation than language.

It is important, therefore, to know how to read the messages associated with time in other cultures. In France almost everything is polychronic whereas in Germany monochronic promptness is even more important than it is in the United States.

Tempo, Rhythm, and Synchrony

Rhythm is an intangible but important aspect of time. Because nature's cycles are rhythmic, it is understandable that rhythm and tempo are distinguishing features of any culture. Rhythm ties the people of a culture together and can also alienate them from members of other cultures. In some cultures people move very slowly; in others, they move rapidly. When people from two such different cultures meet, they are apt to have difficulty relating because they are not "in sync." This is important because synchrony—the subtle ability to move together—is vital to all collaborative efforts, be they conferring, administering, working together on machines, or buying and selling.

People who move at a fast tempo are often perceived as "tailgating" those who move more slowly, and tailgating doesn't contribute to harmonious interaction—nor does forcing fast-paced people to move too slowly. Americans complain that the Germans take forever to reach decisions. Their time is out of phase with American time and vice versa. One must always be contexted to the local time system. There will be times when everything seems to be at a standstill, but actually a great deal is going on behind the scenes. Then there will be other times when everything moves at lightning speed and it is necessary to stand aside, to get out of the way.

Scheduling and Lead Time

To conduct business in an orderly manner in other countries, it is essential to know how much or how little lead time is required for each activity: how far ahead to request an appointment or schedule meetings and vacations, and how much time to allow for the preparation of a major report. In both the United States and Germany, schedules are sacred; in France scheduling frequently cannot be initiated until meetings are held with concerned members of the organization to permit essential discussions. This system works well in France, but there are complications whenever overseas partners or participants are involved since they have often scheduled their own activities up to two years in advance.

Lead time varies from culture to culture and is itself a communication as well as an element in organization. For instance, in France, if the relationship is important, desks will be cleared when that person arrives, whether there has been any advance notice or not. Time will be made to work together, up to twenty-four hours a day if necessary. In the United States and to some extent in Germany, on the other hand, the amount of lead time can be read as an index of the relative importance of the business to be conducted, as well as of the status of the individuals concerned. Short lead time means that the business is of little importance; the longer the lead time, the greater the value of the proceedings. In these countries, two weeks is the minimum advance time for requesting appointments. In Arab countries, two weeks may be too long—a date set so far in advance "slides off their minds"; three or four days may be preferable. In Japan lead time is usually much shorter than in the United States, and it is difficult to say how many conferences on important subjects, attended by all the most competent and prestigious Japanese leaders in their fields, fail to attract suitable counterparts from the United States because of the short lead time. Although misunderstandings are blameless artifacts of the way two very different systems work, accidents of culture are seldom understood for what they are.

Another instance of time as communication is the practice of setting a date to end something. For example, Americans often schedule how long they will stay in a foreign country for a series of meetings, thus creating the psychological pressure of having to arrive at a decision by a certain date. *This is a mistake.* The Japanese and, to a lesser degree, the French are very aware of the American pressure of being "under the gun" and will use it to their advantage during negotiations.

The Importance of Proper Timing

Choosing the correct timing of an important event is crucial. Politicians stake their careers on it. In government and business alike, announcements of major changes or new programs must be carefully timed. The significance of different time segments of the day also must be considered. Certain times of the day, month, or year are reserved for certain activities (vacations, meal times, etc.) and are not ordinarily interchangeable. In general in northern European cultures and in the United States, anything that occurs outside of business hours, very early in the morning, or late at night suggests an emergency. In France there are times when nothing is expected to happen, such as national holidays and during the month of August, when everything shuts down for *vacances.* Culturally patterned systems are sufficiently complex so that it is wise to seek the advice of local experts.

In the U.S. the short business lunch is common and the business dinner rarer; this is not so in France, where the function of the business lunch and dinner is to create the proper atmosphere and get acquainted. Relaxing with business clients during lunch and after work is crucial to building the close rapport that is absolutely necessary if one is to do business.

Appointments

The way in which time is treated by Americans and Germans signals attitude, evaluation of priorities, mood, and status. Since time is highly valued in both Germany and the United States, the messages of time carry more weight than they do in polychronic countries. Waiting time, for example, carries strong messages which work on that part of the brain that mobilizes the emotions (the lymbic systems). In the U.S. only those people with very high status can keep others waiting and get away with it. In general those individuals are the very ones who know enough of human relations to avoid "insults of time" whenever possible. It is the petty bureaucrat who likes to throw his weight around, the bully who takes pleasure in putting people down, or the insecure executive with an inflated ego who keeps visitors waiting. The waiting-room message is a double-edged sword. Not only does it communicate an attitude towards the visitor, but it reveals a lot about the individual who has kept a visitor waiting. In monochronic cultures such as those in the U.S. and Germany, keeping others waiting can be a deliberate putdown or a signal that the individual is very disorganized and can't keep to a schedule. In polychronic cultures such as those of France or Hispanic countries, no such message is intended. In other words, one's reading of the message should be tempered by the context, the realities of the situation, and not with an automatic projection of one's own culture.

Clearly, interactions between monochronic and polychronic people can be stressful unless both parties know and can decode the meanings behind each other's language of time. The language of time is much more stable and resistant to change than other cultural systems. We were once involved in a research project in New Mexico, conducting interviews with Hispanics.

Our subjects were sixth- and seventh-generation descendants of the original Spanish families who settled in North America in the early seventeenth century. Despite constant contact with Anglo-Saxon Americans for well over a hundred years, most of these Hispanics have remained polychronic. In three summers of interviewing we never once achieved our scheduled goal of five interviews each week for each interviewer. We were lucky to have two or three. Interviews in Hispanic homes or offices were constantly interrupted when families came to visit or a friend dropped by. The Hispanics seemed to be juggling half a dozen activities simultaneously, even while the interviews were in progress.

Since we are monochronic Anglo-Saxons, this caused us no little concern and considerable distress. It is hard not to respond emotionally when the rules of your own time system are violated. Nor was an intellectual understanding of the problem much help at first. We did recognize, however, that what we were experiencing was a consequence of cultural differences and was, therefore, a part of our data. This led us to a better understanding of the importance as well as the subtleties of information flow and information networks in a polychronic society.

INFORMATION FLOW: IS IT FAST OR SLOW AND WHERE DOES IT GO?

The rate of information flow is measured by how long it takes a message intended to produce an action to travel from one part of an organization to another and for that message to release the desired response. Cultural differences in information flow are often the greatest stumbling blocks to international understanding. Every executive doing business in a foreign land should know how information is handled—where it goes and whether it flows easily through the society and the business organization, or whether it is restricted to narrow channels because of compartmentalization.

In low-context countries, such as the United States, Germany, and Switzerland, information is highly focused, compartmentalized, and controlled, and, therefore, not apt to flow freely. In high-context cultures, such as the French, the Japanese, and the Spanish, information spreads rapidly and moves almost as if it had a life of its own. Those who use information as an instrument of "command and control" and who build their planning on controlling information are in for a rude shock in societies where people live in a sea of information.

In high-context cultures, interpersonal contact takes precedence over everything else; wherever people are spatially involved with each other, information flows freely. In business, executives do not seal themselves off behind secretaries and closed doors; in fact in Japan senior executives may even share offices so that each person knows as much about the entire base of operations as possible, and in France an executive will have ties to a centrally located bureau chief to keep a finger on the pulse of information flow. In these cultures most people are already highly contexted and therefore don't need to be briefed in much detail for each transaction; the emphasis is on stored rather than on transmitted information. Furthermore, channels are seldom overloaded because people stay in constant contact; therefore, the organizational malady of "information overload" is rare. Schedules and screening (as in the use of private offices) are minimized because they interfere with this vital contact. For high-context people, there are two primary expectations: to context everybody in order to open up the information channels and determine whether the group can work together and to appraise the chances of coming to an agreement in the future. The drive to stay in touch and to keep up to date in high-context cultures is very strong. Because these cultures are also characteristically high-information-flow cultures, being out of touch means to cease to exist as a viable human being.

Organizations where information flows slowly are familiar to both Americans and northern Europeans because low-flow information is associated with both low-context and monochronic time resulting from the compartmentalization associated with low-context institutions and of taking up one thing at a time. In the United States information flows slowly because each executive has a private office and a secretary to serve as a guard so that the executive is not distracted by excessive information. Since executive territory is jealously guarded, American executives often do not share information with their staff or with other department heads. We were once hired as consultants to a large government bureaucracy in which there were problems. Our study revealed multiple causes, the most important of which was a bottleneck created by a high-ranking bureaucrat who managed to block practically all the information going from the top down and from the bottom up. Once the problem had been identified, an agency staff director remarked, "I see we have a blockage in information." In a high-context situation everyone would have already known that this was the case. In a low-context system, however, it was necessary to call in outside consultants to make explicit what some people had suspected but were unable or unwilling to identify.

ACTION CHAINS:
THE IMPORTANCE OF COMPLETION

An action chain is an established sequence of events in which one or more people participate—and contribute—to achieve a goal. It's like the old-fashioned ritual of courtship with its time-honored developmental stages. If either party rushes things too much, omits an important procedure, or delays too long between steps, the courtship grinds to a halt.

Business is replete with action chains: greeting people, hiring and training personnel, developing an advertising campaign, floating a stock offering, initiating a lawsuit, merging with or taking over other companies, even sinking a golf putt. Many bureaucratic procedures are based unconsciously on the action-chain model. Because of the diversity of functions, it may be difficult for some people to link all these activities in their minds,

24

but the common thread of underlying, ordered sequence ties each case to the others.

Because the steps in the chain are either technical (as in floating a stock offering or completing a merger) or else so widely shared and taken for granted that little conscious attention is paid to the details, the need to reexamine the entire pattern has largely gone unrecognized in the overseas setting.

There are important rules governing the structure, though not the content, of action chains. If an important step is left out, the action must begin all over again. Too many meetings and reports, for example, can break the action chains of individual projects, making it difficult for people to complete their work. In fact the breaking of an action chain is one of the most troublesome events with which human beings have to contend in our speeded-up technological twentieth century.

All planning must take into account the elaborate hierarchy of action chains. Monochronic, low-context cultures, with their compartmentalized approach and dependence on scheduled activities, are particularly sensitive to interruptions and so are more vulnerable to the breaking of action chains than high-context cultures. Most Americans are brought up with strong drives to complete action chains. High-context people, because of their intense involvement with each other and their extensive, cohesive networks, are more elastic; there is more "give" in their system. Some polychronic peoples will break an action chain simply because they don't like the way things are going or because they think they can "get a better deal." For instance, we once knew a monochronic architect in New York who was designing a building for a polychronic client. The client continually changed the specifications for the building. With each change, the building design had to be revised, even down to alterations in the building's foundations. The architect found this process particularly devastating because designing and constructing a building is an incredibly complex and elaborate collection of action chains. Changing one thing is likely to throw everything else out of gear.

25

The relationship between action chains and disputes is important. All cultures have built-in safeguards—even though they may not always work—to prevent a dispute from escalating to an out-and-out battle. Keep in mind, however, that these safeguards apply only within the context of one's own culture. In any foreign situation where a dispute appears imminent, it is essential to do two things immediately: proceed slowly, taking every action possible to maintain course and stay on an even keel; and seek the advice of a skillful, tactful interpreter of the culture.

INTERFACING:
CREATING THE PROPER FIT

The concept of interfacing can be illustrated by a simple example: it is impossible to interface an American appliance with a European outlet without an adaptor and a transformer. Not only are the voltages different, but the contacts on one are round; on the other, thin and flat. The purpose of this book is to serve as an adaptor for business executives operating at the interfaces between American, French, and German cultures.

The problems to be solved when interfacing vary from company to company, but some generalizations are possible.

First, it is more difficult to succeed in a foreign country than at home.

Second, the top management of a foreign subsidiary is crucial to the success of interfacing. Therefore, it is important to send the very best people available, take their advice, and leave them alone. Expect that your foreign manager or representative will start explaining things in terms of the local mentality which may sound alien and strange.

Cultural interfacing follows five basic principles:

1. The higher the context of either the culture or the industry, the more difficult the interface;

2. The greater the complexity of the elements, the more difficult the interface;

3. The greater the cultural distance, the more difficult the interface;

4. The greater the number of levels in the system, the more difficult the interface;

5. Very simple, low-context, highly evolved, mechanical systems tend to produce fewer interface problems than multiple-level systems of great complexity that depend on human talent for their success.

An example of an easy-to-interface business would be the manufacture of small components for microscopes by two divisions, one in Germany, the other in Switzerland. The cultural distance in this case is not great since both cultures are low-context as well as monochronic, and the business operation itself does not involve different levels of complexity.

A difficult-to-interface enterprise would be a newspaper or magazine in two countries that are vastly different, such as France and the United States. Publishing is a high-context enterprise which must be neatly meshed at literally dozens of points, including writing, advertising, and editorial policy. The success of newspapers and magazines depends on writers and editors who understand their audience's culture and know how to reach their readers.

RELEASING THE RIGHT RESPONSES

The Importance of Context and Following the Rules

The key to being an effective communicator is in knowing the degree of information (contexting) that must be supplied. If you're communicating with a German, remember she or he is low-context and will need lots of information and all the details, in depth. If you're communicating with someone from France, she or he is high-context and won't require as much information. Here are two examples from our interviews:

One German manager working for a French firm was fired after his first year because he didn't perform as expected. The German manager was stunned. His response was, "But nobody told me what they wanted me to do."

The opposite problem was encountered by a Frenchman who resigned from a German firm because he was constantly being told what he already knew by his German superior. Both his intelligence and his pride were threatened.

In both situations, the executives were inept at releasing the right response from their subordinates.

One of the factors that determines whether one releases the right response includes observing the rules of the other culture, including the time system. In Germany a salesman can have a very fine presentation, but if he arrives late by even a few minutes, no one will be impressed, no matter how good it is. Indeed, in all probability, the Germans will not even wait around to hear it. In France form is preeminent; without it, no message can release the right response. Americans must take great care not to alienate the French by being casual and informal in their manners; if Americans are not meticulously polite and formal, their message will not get through to the French, and they and their product will suffer.

The Importance of the Right Interpreter

Releasing the right response will also depend on choosing the right interpreter. An interpreter's accent or use of the local dialect can cause a negative reaction. The importance of this facet of communication cannot be overstressed, yet it is one of the most frequent violations of the unwritten laws of communication abroad. For example, if you are trying to communicate with a Japanese executive using an interpreter who is not well educated nor extremely polite and proper, the desired response from the Japanese will not be forthcoming. A well-educated and well-mannered interpreter whose use of the language reflects a good background is also highly desirable in France and Germany.

SUMMARY

Speed of messages, context, space, time, information flow, action chains, and interfacing are all involved in the creation of both national and corporate character. In organizations everything management does communicates; when viewed in the cultural context, all acts, all events, all material things have meaning. Some organizations send strong, consistent messages that are readily grasped by employees and customers alike. Other organizations are less easy to interpret; they do not communicate clearly, or their messages are incongruent. Sometimes one part of the organization communicates one thing and another part communicates something else. The cues around which these corporate and cultural messages are organized are as different as the languages with which they are associated. Most important, their meaning is deeply imbedded and therefore harder for management to change when making the transition from one country to another.

Many messages are implied or have a cultural meaning, and there is a tacit agreement as to the nature of that meaning which is deeply rooted in the context of the communication. There is much that is taken for granted in culture that few people can explain but which every member of the culture accepts as given. Remember that messages come in many forms (most of them not in words) which are imbedded in the context and in the choice of channels.

Within all cultures there are important unstated differences as to what constitutes a proper *releaser.* Our research over the years in choosing the correct releaser has indicated that people cluster around preferences for "words," "numbers," and "pictures." Using the wrong format (sending numbers when words are wanted, words when the recipient only feels comfortable with numbers, or words and/or numbers to the visually-oriented person) can only release a negative, frustrated response. The fascinating thing is that the message can be the same in every case. Furthermore, it is quite evident that each culture has its own preferences in this regard.

A television ad that is effective in the United States will have to be translated into a print media message to reach Germans. Germans are print-oriented, which explains in part why there is so little advertising on German TV. Also, Germans are always looking for what is "true" and to them numbers are a way of signaling that a product is exactly as it has been represented. Germans demand facts, facts, and more facts.

It is not uncommon for Americans to experience difficulty getting the French—even those whom they know and have done business with—to reply to inquiries, even urgent ones. This can be exasperating. The reasons are many but most have to do with the importance of immediate human contacts to the French. A solution that succeeds when other methods fail is to use a surrogate to relay messages rather than relying on a letter or a phone call. Why? Because letters and telephone calls aren't personal enough. If you send a properly placed emissary, one whom the individual you are trying to reach likes and trusts and considers important, you add the necessary personal touch to your message and will thereby release the right response.

The French also stress the importance of observing the many rituals of form. If you don't use the right form, the message conveyed is that you are ignorant or ill-mannered or don't care. In any event, the response that is released is almost certain to be negative. Remember that the French deplore casualness and informality. Paying attention to the details and being correct in everything you do is the only tactic that releases the right response in France.

It is not necessary to solve every problem at once, only to show a genuine desire to do so and to take one step at a time, even if it seems to take a lifetime. The rewards are not only material but psychological and mental as well. New frontiers are not only to be found in outer space or in the microworld of science; they are also at the interfaces between cultures.

PART 2

The Germans

Like most countries, West Germany has many regional differences; most significantly, there are many distinct differences between northern Germany and southern Germany. (Munich is not Mannheim, especially in work ethic and time system). When we use the term *German* we refer to those West Germans who inhabit industrialized areas of the north in such centers as Frankfurt, Düsseldorf, Köln, Stuttgart, and Hamburg. Most American business firms work with Germans in this geographic area and this is where we conducted our interviews. We are not referring to the people of southern Germany, nor are we referring to East Germans.

GERMAN CULTURE

German Time: Precise Scheduling, Slow Pace

Time lies at the core of German culture. For Germans it is one of the principal ways of organizing life. In general German time and American time are both monochronic and follow the same basic patterns. However, there are some subtle but crucial differences.

Germans are very high on the monochronic scale, and their consensus decision-making process is often more involved and deliberate than the American, requiring many lateral clearances as well as considerable extensive background research. Because the Germans approach decision making slowly and laboriously, once a decision is made they stand firmly and unalterably behind it. Be warned: changing plans after things are in place may strike Germans as arbitrary and irresponsible. While most Americans are monochronic, some are not and think nothing of changing plans at the last minute. When this happens, it is difficult for their German business associates to accept; they become upset and sometimes enraged.

Promptness is taken for granted in Germany—in fact, it's almost an obsession. If there is a chance you'll be late for an appointment, telephone ahead. The Germans want to know where their expected visitors are at all times; not knowing where to reach a visitor violates the German sense of order.

German time and German consciousness are steeped in the past. When they explain something, they often find it necessary to lay a proper foundation and as a result are apt to go back to Charlemagne. Such lengthy explanations make the average American impatient and drive the French crazy.

This anecdote illustrates the German obsession with detail and their preoccupation with the past:

Once upon a time, journalists from all over the world were asked to write a story about the elephant. The Frenchman wrote *L'elé-phant et l'amour*. The American wrote *Thirty-seven Miracle Diets*

35

and the Modern Working Elephant. And the German wrote *The Socio-Dynamic Nature and Fundamental Psychological Constitution of the Elephant: Volume I, The Burmese Ceremonial Elephant,* Chapter 1, "From Karl the Great to the Present."

For those interested in background reading, historian Gordon A. Craig has written an excellent book, *The Germans,* and Flora Lewis has a helpful chapter on West Germany in her book, *Europe.* Also, Henry Ashby Turner, in *German Big Business and the Rise of Hitler,* presents a fascinating account of the relations between business and the Third Reich (see reading list).

The German preoccupation with historical context brings up the matter of pace. Everything from the answer to a question to the length of tenure for German chancellors lasts two to four times as long as it does in the United States. Because decision making in Germany requires seemingly interminable discussion, a slow response to a business proposal does not necessarily mean lack of interest. Bide your time and, if you have access to them, try outside information channels to find out the status of your proposal.

The slower German pace can affect day-to-day life. We have heard dozens of stories from foreigners who made major purchases in Germany of furniture or appliances and had to wait months for delivery. One Japanese banker told us of ordering a dining room set from one of the best furniture manufacturers in Germany. His order was placed in September, and he was told delivery would be in six weeks. When he inquired at the end of October, he was told brusquely that the furniture had not arrived; no other information was forthcoming. By Christmas the furniture had still not arrived. It finally arrived at the end of March. Even though the Germans place a great deal of emphasis on promptness, delays in areas such as deliveries do occur, probably because of the extreme compartmentalization of German life and business. It is possible for a salesperson to take an order, then leave for vacation and not ask anyone else to follow up on the order. Problems in shipping from a manufacturer are not conveyed to the retailer and the customer. This

36

compartmentalization can slow down other kinds of business transactions as well.

German businesses plan for the future, methodically building a solid foundation. They are not preoccupied with immediate results. Most German companies are not publicly owned and therefore have no need to provide stock analysts with quarterly reports of growth and profits. It is important for Germans to complete action chains, and so they find it inconvenient and disruptive to be asked for quarterly financial statements and reports; instead, they provide annual financial reports. In some German industries, five years is not considered long-term and many companies routinely plan ten and twenty years ahead.

Tempo, pace, compartmentalized monochronic time with its great emphasis on scheduling—all combine to create great differences in tempo between German and American business. The slow pace is hard on Americans, who must constantly remind themselves that Germans resent being tailgated.

It is necessary for Americans to remind themselves that their senses and judgment are not always reliable in a foreign environment, even after months or years. Prolonged and intimate contact between monochronic Germans and polychronic people such as the French does little to change the behavior of either group. It is difficult for polychronic people to accept the importance of schedules and the extreme compartmentalization in monochronic culture. Polychronic people, as we mentioned earlier, adhere to a time system that emphasizes involvement with people and minimizes scheduling and compartmentalization. When a polychronic Frenchman is late to a meeting, the monochronic German is likely to misinterpret the tardiness as irresponsibility, egocentricity, or rudeness.

German Space: Inviolate

Americans are highly mobile geographically, socially, and economically and by necessity have developed strategies for interacting with strangers. Germany is not a melting-pot society and Germans are not mobile. Many have stayed in the same geographic region and even the same house for generations and have had little interaction with foreigners. Unlike Americans, they are not used to meeting and interacting with strangers at home. As a result, they treat the *Auslander* with a certain wariness. The guest workers *(Gastarbeiter)* from Turkey, Yugoslavia, Italy, Pakistan, and Greece remain isolated and unassimilated (this is true largely for the first generation of immigrants). The largest group are the Turks, who seek to maintain their own culture and religion and live in ethnic enclaves, and they have done very little intermingling with the Germans. In fact it is very distressing to the Germans that the Turks do not show signs of wanting to become acculturated. During a recent recession in Germany, efforts were made to encourage guest workers to return to their own countries, but these efforts were unsuccessful, which created resentment in some Germans since jobs were in short supply. And since unemployment remains high, the tension persists.

The scale of everything is smaller in Germany than in the United States. Many Germans feel hemmed in geographically. They love the outdoors and open spaces and treasure their forests. Hiking is a popular national sport. Germans who visit the United States comment on how impressed they are with the vast amount of space, particularly in the West. Conversely, Americans find German houses, apartments, and even appliances inconveniently small.

Although the Germans and Americans share a significant part of each other's culture, they clash on the handling of space. For the German, *space is sacred.* Their sense of being geographically crowded is a contributor to this territorial behavior. Homes are protected from outsiders by a variety of barriers: fences, walls, hedges, solid doors, blinds, shutters, and screening to prevent visual or auditory intrusion. Front yards are beautifully maintained but rarely used, and residential streets often appear deserted. Outside activities—sitting in the sun or visiting with family—are restricted to the back yard, away from the street and the eyes of others. The German's home is a castle and a refuge from the outside world. It is the most important possession, and life in the home with one's family is treasured.

Any invitation to visit a German home is an honor. Germans seldom invite anyone who is not a close friend, and an invitation may be a signal that they wish to explore the possibility of becoming friends. By all means accept graciously and arrive promptly, with a small bouquet for the hostess (not red roses, which convey romantic attachments), which you should unwrap before presenting.

The German sense of privacy is much stronger than the American. Germans respect each other's privacy to a degree far beyond anything known in the United States. Learn what is considered personal and do not ask questions that may be offensive. It's possible to live in a German neighborhood for years without forming a close relationship with one's neighbors. They may nod or greet each other briefly, always with formality, when they meet, but they don't expect to chat across the hedge or in the hallways of apartment buildings, and they don't borrow things from each other (it's a breach of etiquette to admit to having run out of something). When Americans move to Germany, they often feel isolated because they miss interacting with neighbors as they did at home, and they perceive German behavior as unfriendly.

Within the German home, family members abide by formal rules of behavior designed to give one another distance and privacy. These patterns of formality extend in adulthood to relations with friends and coworkers in the office. German friends of many years continue to address each other by their last names: "Herr Schmidt," not "Walter."

Germans are careful not to touch accidentally or to encourage signs of intimacy. On the other hand, they do maintain direct eye contact in conversations to show they are paying attention. Americans often comment on the fact that Germans do not smile when introduced. Smiling is for friends. Gestures are also restrained. Their handshake is firm and they look directly at you. Germans may appear stiff, distant, and even forbidding to

Americans. But remember that a reserved nature should not be mistakenly interpreted as a lack of friendliness.

In Germany intrusion distance (the distance people must stand from each other to feel comfortable) is greater than in the United States. To Americans, German furniture appears too far apart for comfortable conversation, but Germans feel that moving the chairs in someone else's home or office, a common American habit, is intrusive and officious. Fortunately, German furniture is usually so heavy it discourages such adjustments.

Most important, the German concept of visual intrusion is entirely different from that of the American. The Germans consider looking into a room from the outside as an intrusion into the room itself; hence, you must respect the actual physical interior of a room by never entering without permission. And a person standing at the threshold of a room is considered to be inside the room. You must also keep your eyes to yourself. Germans think it rude to look at strangers in public or to photograph strangers in public without their permission (in some places there were once laws against it).

The Door As Symbol: A Solid Barrier

In Germany there are books written about nothing but doors. The German's space is sacred and vigorously defended; therefore, the importance of the door in Germany cannot be overemphasized. Psychologically, the door stands as a protective barrier between the individual and the outside world. When the door is closed, the compartment is sealed and one is safe. Rooms in hotels and other public buildings often have double doors. Doors are thick and solid, their hardware heavy, tight-fitting, and built to close tolerances—no cracks to peek through for the Germans.

One American manufacturer who had acquired a German company discovered that in the company headquarters each of the executives had a private office with double doors and soundproof walls. The American officials assumed the German officers wanted to keep secrets from their peers. But what the doors and soundproofing really meant was that each officer was responsible for her or his own department and that the officer ran that department without group consultation (compartmentalization again).

Germans keep doors closed. When you encounter a closed door, knock and wait to be invited to enter. The closed door preserves the integrity of the room, provides a boundary between people, and minimizes eavesdropping, interruptions, and accidental intrusions. In business the closed door also means that a supervisor respects the privacy of subordinates and is not looking over their shoulders.

Power: The Name of the Game

Power is the name of the game in German business. In Germany, as in any country, the businessperson must learn to recognize where power resides and how it is used. Real power is more visible in Germany than in the United States, and Germans are adept at "sniffing it out" in business relationships. They are also very quick to discover when it is *not* present. In business, power flows from the top down and moves very slowly through many layers of management. Germans understand and use power in negotiations and have a reputation for being hard bargainers. In the words of an experienced American banker:

> You must be absolutely firm in your resolve and hold to your position. Meet force with force. Germans understand power and they are also very tough to deal with. They play hard ball.

Since knowledge is power, secrecy is common. Germans do not share information freely, and it is difficult to get information in most organizations.

Power can be financial, political, entrepreneurial, managerial, or intellectual. Of the five, intellectual power seems to rank highest in Germany, which is why many heads of German firms have doctoral degrees (and those who do are always addressed as "Doctor").

41

As one might expect, material possessions, social position, and professional level all symbolize power. People of power and authority in German business have the usual accoutrements of success—large offices, expensive automobiles, and handsome homes. They also often have a demeanor that communicates decisiveness and strength of personality. They are physically imposing in posture and bearing, polished in manners, and impressive in the breadth of their knowledge.

As in the United States, power is reflected in the location, furnishings, and style of offices. Because Americans share these symbols, they can interpret German power indicators with reasonable accuracy. A corner office means the same thing in Germany as it does in the United States. In new buildings the offices are generally lavish by U.S. standards, working conditions for middle- and lower-level personnel are excellent, and German offices for upper management tend to be larger.

There is one crucial difference between German and American ideas of success: Germans usually prefer that power and position be handled with grace and reserve. Americans in positions of power are often much more ostentatious in their material possessions and in their enthusiasm for publicity about their lavish lifestyles.

Certain signals of rank are very important to German executives, and courtesies should be carefully observed. For example, one visiting American VIP was touring a company factory. The factory general manager always insisted that the VIP walk on his right during the plant tours. Similarly, the sales manager wanted the VIP to sit on his right while driving through the countryside in a chauffeured car. The right is the position of respect. A senior officer of a company or a distinguished visitor must go through every door first while it is held open by the host officer or executive. German men enter restaurants ahead of women, and the man walks on the left side of the woman on the street.

In a meeting or in personal discussions, the German who speaks most softly and to whom others defer is the one to pay attention to, not the one who makes the most noise.

42

Americans who ignore these signals of rank, status, and protocol in an effort to appear egalitarian and friendly will only upset their German hosts.

Order in All Things

Order is a dominant theme in German culture. In Germany there is order in all things. In handling space, Germans insist on well-defined, well-ordered territories with boundaries that are carefully protected since they are very sensitive to spatial intrusions. (One exception to orderliness is German behavior in lines for service; in stores, at ticket counters, or in boarding planes, especially where there is no seat assignment, Germans do not form queues but instead crowd and push and can be very rough. They do not yield when someone says "Excuse me." Their determination to be served overrides their usual need to avoid physical contact.)

Germans prefer doing one thing at a time and keeping each activity discrete. This means schedules are scrupulously observed and appointments kept promptly. Germans expect or ganization and order in all things—especially business presentations, which should be well thought out, carefully researched, thorough, and orderly. None of this drive for order, however, prevents Germans from being creative. Germany has a rich, creative tradition in art, music, and literature.

German procedures work both as a management tool and as a way to correct mistakes. Often, if a problem develops, the procedure is assumed to be at fault and a new procedure is adopted, even though a change in procedure does not always solve the problem. In monochronic cultures such as Germany and the United States, where people are often subordinated to procedures, managers often fail to take into account human needs and human behavior. German procedures are more inclusive and complex and even less responsive to human needs than are American procedures.

The sense of order reinforces a strong drive for conformity, and therefore, the Germans object strenuously when people fail to obey signs and directions. Become familiar with most common German signs: *Geschlossen* (closed), *Kein Zutritt* (no entry), *Ruhe* (silence), *Nicht Rauchen* (no smoking). Obey them.

Compartmentalization: Airtight

Decentralization and compartmentalization are basic, prominent structural features of German culture at all levels of society, from the individual at home or in the office to the organization of the business hierarchy right up to the national level. Germany was unified as a country under Bismark in 1871, rather late in its history. Before unification it had already developed strong urban concentrations which have continued as centers of power and influence. Today Germany has no one center: no Tokyo, Paris, or Rome. Although Bonn is the capital, there are many cities of greater importance; Frankfurt, Düsseldorf, Hamburg, and Stuttgart are all important financial and commercial hubs. This dispersion of power reflects the German preference for an organizational structure without a center.

Following World War II Germany was divided into two countries: East Germany (*Deutsche Democratische Republik*— German Democratic Republic) and West Germany (*Bundesrepublik Deutschland*—Federal Republic of Germany). This division compartmentalized life further for the Germans. One of the most unfortunate results of this political division was the isolation of Berlin, which had been Germany's former capital. Before World War II Berlin was a city of enormous importance to Germans, not only politically and economically, but as a center for literature, art, music, and the theater as well.

The first thing Americans notice when working with Germans is that their extreme compartmentalization rules everything. Germans compartmentalize time with appointments and schedules to which they adhere faithfully; they compartmentalize space by sealing themselves off from other people behind closed double doors to discourage interruptions and ensure privacy for concentration. This compartmentalized view of the world blocks the free flow of information and can create serious problems in

44

business. Germans do not share information freely except with their own particular work group, and sometimes not even with them. Inevitably, decisions are often made without benefit of vital information. This highly restricted information flow is probably the greatest handicap for Germans in business.

The children learn compartmentalization early. Schools are compartmentalized and only academic subjects are taught. There are no athletic clubs, no after-school programs, and no integration of school into the activities of the community. After class, teachers go home and children are responsible for doing their homework.

The educational system does offer excellent public schools, open to all, from which it is possible to go on to universities (many of which, unfortunately, are overcrowded and under-funded). The competition for university admission is fierce and is based solely on scholastic achievement. There are no special private schools that wield great influence for university admission as there are in France. There is little contact between business and universities, which is unfortunate since universities are the source of many of the scientific and technological breakthroughs needed by German business.

Geographic decentralization and universal compartmentalization combine to produce a society of multiple and independent units. There is a paucity of informal information networks cutting across organizational boundaries in Germany. As a result, changes can occur without the public even knowing about them. Since this can lead to serious social crises, the German public is especially dependent on a responsible, free press.

Possessions: Having vs. Using

The material goods produced by any culture reveal underlying attitudes and values that are clues to understanding the psychology of its people. It would be hard to find a greater contrast between Germans and Americans than in their attitudes toward possessions.

Status and prestige are attached to material possessions in both countries. However, the American attitude is that things are meant to be *used*; if they serve no useful purpose, we dispose of them. The German attitude is that things have great intrinsic value. Take books, for example. Americans often feel remiss if they buy books and don't read them. But a German will feel that it is important to own a book even if one can't read it immediately. Sales of hardcover books in Germany exceed sales of paperbacks; in the United States the opposite is true.

Germans believe that their possessions have inherent value, symbolizing permanence in an unstable, fast-moving world. Germans have lived through several cataclysmic events, including two devastating wars, with a ruinous inflation between the wars; it is understandable that they should cling to possessions, with their promise of enduring value.

Germans also expect things to look and feel solid and to last a long time. In fact, their term for solid (*solide)* means much more than it does in the United States. *Solide* connotes reliability and character. People who are upstanding and dependable are *solide.*

The Germans give their material possessions hard use. On the *Autobahn*, for example, many drive at top speed—over one hundred miles per hour—for hours at a time. They don't pamper either people or things—both are supposed to have the strength, discipline, and control to be able to take it.

Associated with their demand for high-quality, long-lasting goods is the German abhorrence of waste. Waste is a sin. Germans do not understand how Americans can waste so much energy by heating, cooling, and lighting buildings at levels that are obviously excessive. The American practice of illuminating high-rise office buildings at night is incomprehensible to Germans; they illuminate only the top floor or the business name or logo on their own highrises, and even those lights are shut off late at night.

Germans are value-conscious and always insist on getting their money's worth. This concern with quality and upkeep has implications for American business. Don't ever try to sell goods

46

that are less than high quality on the German market. The Germans appreciate—in fact, demand—fine workmanship, excellent design, and high-quality materials. They expect things to wear well.

German cars such as Mercedes and BMW are known throughout the world for their high quality. In Germany you can own one with peace of mind and satisfaction because German mechanics understand these machines and know how to keep them running perfectly. Mechanics take great pride in their work and rarely have to be asked to do a job twice. Other German products, such as Leitz lenses and Leica cameras, are considered among the best in the world; the items may cost a fortune, but they last a lifetime.

Along with pride of ownership comes a concern for upkeep. German homes are spotless and gleaming and well maintained both inside and out. The German housewife works very hard and is a systematic, efficient homemaker. If you live in Germany, you may be called on by your neighbors if your windows aren't washed and polished each week or if your lawn needs mowing. Anything that detracts from the overall appearance of the neighborhood will bring an immediate negative response. Each neighborhood has its own informal rules about when you can wash your car, when you hang out your laundry, when and where you put out the trash for collection, and where you can walk the dogs. You will be constantly policed by your German neighbors. German neighbors also dislike any noise that disturbs them, especially during the night. Be forewarned.

The German feeling of territoriality extends to automobiles and other possessions. Their automobiles are immaculate, shining, and perfectly maintained, and they don't want anyone to put a finger on them. When parking, they are meticulous; even a tap on a bumper is considered serious enough to call the police. Be sure that you and your family (including your children) do not touch or do anything to disturb or damage the property of others.

Germans also feel strongly about not borrowing possessions. Never use anything that belongs to a German without first asking

47

permission, and avoid borrowing altogether if possible. This attitude is in direct conflict with American patterns of informality and sharing in both the office and personal life.

Formality: Politeness and Distance

Despite two world wars and the attendant economic and social upheaval, remnants of a class system still exist in Germany, especially at the top levels of business.

The old German aristocracy is still a factor to be reckoned with. These upper-class families are a very proud group with high standards. Following World War II, many of them were destitute. The males had either been killed or seriously wounded; the women who survived, determined to give their children an education, took any jobs they could get, even scrubbing floors for American servicemen. They lived on nothing and saved their money. Many of their children are prominent in Germany today. The tradition of hard work, discipline, self-sacrifice, and education should be a familiar theme to students of American history.

One obvious vestige of the class system in Germany is the emphasis on good manners. Educated, responsible people are expected to display good manners, especially in business or when interacting with people they know. For the American in Germany, manners will be a most important asset.

American informality and the habit of calling others by their first names make Germans acutely uncomfortable, particularly when young people or people lower in the hierarchy address their elders or their superiors by their first names. *The taboo against first-naming should not be dismissed as an empty convention.* It takes a long time to get on a first-name basis with a German; if you rush the process, you will be perceived as overly friendly and rude.

In the German language, there are two forms of address for *you*, the familiar *du* and the formal *Sie*. *Du* is used only by family members and intimate friends. *Sie* is always used until you are invited to use *du*. There is an old custom (no longer universal) called the *Bruderschafttrinken* (drink to brotherhood), by which

48

two friends formalize their shift to the more intimate form of address. They hook arms and each sips from a glass. Then they shake hands and announce their first names. This custom is a symbol of the German desire for formality and politeness between people and of the great importance of close relationships. Germans are never casual about friendships.

The formal mode of address is *always* used when addressing subordinates. This includes your driver, the janitor, and the doorman. Germans are very conscious of their status and insist on proper forms of address. They are bewildered by the American custom of addressing a new acquaintance by his or her first name and are even more startled by our custom of addressing a superior by first name. In Germany, though there are a few exceptions, the boss will be "Herr Muller" for the duration of the employee's life.

When you meet a German couple, protocol also holds sway. Always be sure you shake hands with the wife before you shake hands with her husband. Otherwise you risk serious offense.

Communication Style

Language is a direct reflection of culture and German is no exception. Just as the verb often comes at the end of a German sentence, it takes a while for Germans to get to the point. Be patient. Americans are accustomed to the headline style—they announce at the start what they are going to talk about. Americans may not always be able to identify a German speaker's main point until the speaker reaches the end of the speech. Because of this difference in communication style, Americans should repeat their main point at the end of a presentation, or the German listener may miss it.

In general Germans provide much more information than most people from other cultures require. As one American engineer said, "They tell you more than you need to know and then some." Many foreigners, especially the French, feel such detailed explanations are a put-down and they dislike the extreme low contexting. "Don't they think we know anything?" is

49

a typical French response to German explanations (also, lengthy explanations take time that the impatient French resent).

Germans value honesty and directness, and they love examples. The term *zum Beispiel* ("for example") is a frequently used phrase. They also like facts, facts, and more facts, and they like written factual texts, as well as figures. They love projections for future events and charts. The figures must be accurate to preserve credibility, though.

Be orderly and logical in outlining your facts. As mentioned above, the summary at the end is key; it should include all your major points, even though you have already covered them earlier. The summary is a good example of the difference between merely sending the right message (your view of your presentation) and releasing the desired response (producing understanding and acceptance in the Germans). Give them all the information you have, and then more. Germans often feel that foreigners provide only sketchy information that leaves out the important minutiae.

The German language is much more literal than English. This means Germans are conditioned from early childhood to be exact in the meaning of words. Each German word has a specific meaning. For example, in English there is one word for "comfort." The Germans have eight, each denoting a slightly different type of comfort. This difference in the precision of meaning of words often leads Germans to think that Americans are careless in their use of language.

The English and German languages are also different in the way they incorporate new technological words. Since the Germans tend toward understatement and are more direct, they use simple terms such as *Fernsprecher* ("far speaker") for telephone and *Fernseher* ("far seer") for television. Americans, on the other hand, mix up Latin and Greek roots to devise words such as *hydromatic, stereophonic, instamatic,* and *teleprompter.*

Germans usually regard concise writing as simple-minded and not worthy of serious consideration. Many highly regarded German authors are noted for their complex, reticulated styles.

The more difficult it is to understand, the more valuable the ideas must be, according to German standards.

Other differences in the use of language also reflect the culture. In general Americans are inclined toward overstatement and like hype, particularly in advertising and promotion; Germans avoid it. Germans think Americans blow things out of proportion as if they are afraid they won't receive enough attention unless they indulge in hyperbole.

Since language is one of the keys to understanding the mentality of a people, any American business involved in the German market will have a distinct advantage by insisting that its principal employees speak German. It is not necessary to be letter-perfect because, unlike the French, the Germans really appreciate a foreigner's making an effort to speak the language. However, and understandably, Germans do feel that if you can't speak the language at all, you really shouldn't be doing business in Germany.

Americans are not used to learning other languages, but we would be more successful and get along better overseas if we were. The following story illustrates how developing mutual understanding is aided by knowing the language:

> The vice president of an American company was visiting one of his company's German factories, which was having a problem with waste, a scrap rate in excess of 20 percent. The American walked the production line, talked with foremen, and watched the workers. He spent several days getting to know the factory manager, speaking to him in German and building a relationship. They spent many hours touring the facility and discussing what they saw there. Finally, the VP brought up the problem of the scrap rate and asked what could be done. The manager suggested the removal of an American production engineer who insisted that everyone do things his way. The VP decided to remove the engineer for a month to see if things improved. When he returned, the scrap rate had dropped to less than half its formal level. The VP knew that he could never have achieved sufficient rapport with the factory manager to get him to criticize the American engineer had he not been able to speak German.

GERMAN PSYCHOLOGY

In Germany, there is as much variation in character, tempera-ment, and personality as one would expect to find anywhere else, but these differences may be difficult to identify at first because of the very strong rules for culturally patterned behav-ior. Germans are apt to present themselves to others in a typically German way, although they do want to be understood and appreciated as individuals, not as "those people." As you will be told repeatedly, Germany is a small country with a population of 60.1 million. In small countries people crowd in on each other, and the need to conform is much greater than in the United States, which stretches across an entire continent. In addition German society is much more homogeneous than American society and the pressure to observe all rules—legal, informal, and formal—is great.

Germans as a whole are quite serious and take themselves very seriously. They certainly don't expect to have fun at work; work is serious business. Don't expect to see them smiling a lot, but remember they are not unfriendly; they are simply much more reserved and serious than Americans. Also, Germans keep to themselves. Their strong feelings of privacy and territoriality give the average American the idea that they are standoffish and do not like to socialize.

Strong pressures to conform in public are ubiquitous. Ger-mans want to be correct in everything they do and therefore hate to make mistakes; they become very upset when they do and sometimes offer excuses or look for a scapegoat. Germans also do not hesitate to tell people when they are out of line since unusual behavior makes them anxious. Germans will correct foreigners' behavior, but they are equally concerned about enforcing proper behavior on each other and constantly correct each other, even strangers, in public.

Germans need to control, as do Americans. The difference is that Germans are more concerned with maintaining institu-tional control and procedures than with individual control

52

within a department. Good managers in German business are those who know how to make the most of individual capabilities within the context of organizational controls and procedures.

Correct behavior is symbolized by appropriate and very conservative dress. The male business uniform is a freshly pressed, dark suit and tie with a plain shirt and dark shoes and socks. It is important to emulate this conservative approach to both manners and dress. Personal appearance, like the exterior appearance of their homes, is very important to Germans.

Some of the rather dour characteristics one sees in Germans are by-products of German seriousness and realism. Germans place a high value on frankness and directness. They want to get beneath the surface to see the underlying truth; they want to see all the facts, the good and the bad. Until they do, they cannot feel secure. They are not afraid of shocking people or of controversy, and investigative journalism is consequently very popular in Germany. German magazines often feature stories that present a "behind-the-scenes" view of malfeasance, crime, and social problems, such as poverty, disease, and violence, in graphic detail. Germans don't find such details disagreeable; they want to see everything for themselves, even those things that are unpleasant.

Along with their directness and frankness goes an absolute absence of what we call social chit-chat. Germans do not "make conversation" at social gatherings; they are serious and dislike small talk. They are also not open to strangers or casual acquaintances—here the contrast between the German and American cultures is extreme.

Germans are stubborn, persistent, and often arrogant. They simply will not give up once they've decided upon a certain course of action, which is one reason for their business successes. However, their stubbornness makes it very difficult for them to take in information, and this, coupled with their compartmentalized approach to life, causes great problems. We were repeatedly told that the biggest single problem of those in overseas operations of German firms is convincing the home office about how business is done in a foreign country. Most often the advice and recommendations from abroad are flatly rejected by the German home office.

Beneath the German's serious and often forbidding exterior is a deep need to be thought well of and respected. Although they value respect much more than popularity, they also want to be liked. German feelings are intense—they don't show much emotion but they do feel it, intensely.

Many observers have noted the melancholy that seems to afflict Germans. Their past hangs over them like a black cloud. Despite their remarkable achievements in rebuilding their cities and the resurgence of a strong economy, there are feelings of pessimism.

German friendships are deeper than anything most Americans have known. In Germany close friends bare their souls to each other and discuss their most private problems and feelings. In-depth philosophical discussions about the meaning of life are also an important part of friendship. While many Germans living in the United States say they enjoy their freedom from the strict bonds of convention, they also miss the close friendships and the warm, long, comfortable discussions they had with their German friends. To Germans, most American friendships are superficial.

Many Germans feel that well-mannered people do not raise their voices. Yet we have heard complaints from Americans and from other Europeans that Germans make too much noise and talk too loudly. This paradox arises because the pressure to conform in Germany is so strong; many Germans need to let off steam occasionally and can be boisterous on occasion.

There will be adjustments for the American in Germany. There will be both positive and negative experiences. An open-minded, optimistic approach is crucial for Americans hoping to find things they genuinely like and admire in German culture. Germans are justly famous for their literature, music, art, and intellectual accomplishments. And there are many other things to admire about German culture: promptness, cleanliness, order, a genuine desire to be fair, candor, directness, perseverance, and determination. We urge Americans planning to live in Germany to study the invaluable handbook *These Strange German Ways,* edited by Irmgard Burmeister.

GERMAN BUSINESS

In recent years West German business has been very successful in the world market. During a time of great uncertainty, German industry has concentrated on producing high-quality goods and on building market share overseas. At the same time many business firms have also expanded their dealer networks. This tripartite strategy has resulted in solid gains in world trade.

The success of German industry has been the result of astute planning and a determination to diversify. At the same time German business has been careful not to become dependent on any one foreign country for its export market or on any one export product. This is particularly important in an era of fluctuating currencies. It is a tribute to the high standards of German goods that West Germany maintained or increased its market share in the United States, even after the dollar fell drastically against the Deutschmark. German industry soon discovered that Americans would pay a premium for top quality goods such as BMW automobiles and Stihl chainsaws.

Much of Germany's success is also due to advanced technology in certain industries. Another significant factor is high capital investment in new plants and equipment, an investment 30 percent higher than in comparable American industries and much greater than in comparable French industries. Recently, German industry has increased spending on basic research and automation to improve its competitive position even more.

Domestically, German business is significantly different from American business. Business customs, the organization of society, the role of labor and government, and the maturity and size of the market in Germany all vary significantly from those aspects of American society. In many respects German business today is reminiscent of business in the United States fifty years ago. We do not mean that it is not up-to-date, but rather that the size and character of German business are reminiscent of American business in the early part of this century.

The small size of some German industries can be an advantage. For example, the German textile industry is small, highly specialized, and responsive to changes in the world market. Most importantly, there are information networks for sharing new technologies among the various German textile firms (which is, admittedly, unusual in German industry). In contrast the American textile industry has huge automated factories in which employees are trained to perform only one job. These factories cannot respond quickly or economically to new technology or changing market conditions. Also, instead of sharing information, they compete unrestrainedly among themselves. As a result, American textile firms are losing market share to the more innovative, responsive, and smaller German textile industry.

The Negative Image of German Business

To Americans, who are accustomed to the high status business enjoys in the United States, it may come as a shock to learn that, in Germany, business has a more negative image and that business executives are often reticent and sometimes almost apologetic about its success. This is mystifying considering that German business has been extremely prosperous during the last forty years, raising the country's standard of living to one of the highest in the world, providing millions of people with good jobs and generous fringe benefits, and giving the country a highly favorable balance of trade. Part of the reason for the negative image comes from a residual resentment of the monopolies that dominated German society and exploited the German worker following World War I. There are also influential political factions, notably Marxists, who are opposed to business on principle. Also, as in many industrial countries, there is widespread concern about damage to the environment from industrial pollution. But there is another, very important factor: German business has little understanding of the concept of corporate image. The leaders of German business eschew publicity. The result is little public awareness of the important role of business in Germany, and business leaders have been slow to make their case.

Individually, it's all right for the German businessperson to be ambitious and successful, though one must never be obvious about it. Since it's bad to stand out, flaunting one's success can be dangerous. Assertiveness in business is permitted, but aggressiveness is considered bad form.

Problems in German Business

Germans make a decision and then they investigate and study all the attendant details. The Japanese study first and then make the decision.

—Japanese banker in Germany

German business often suffers from the arrogance and inflexibility of its leaders, the prolonged decision-making process and, above all, from its extreme compartmentalization which blocks information flow.

There is a sense of complacency in German business. Perhaps it's what Jane Kramer, the *New Yorker* correspondent, describes as the German tendency "to push their fears out of consciousness, to defend themselves against reality with aggressive complacency."

At the top level of business are members of the old German aristocracy. These people are very conscious of their status and position and expect—in fact, demand—great deference from their subordinates. Americans describe them as arrogant. One German manager said that "Germans have a tendency to kick you when they're on top and kiss you when they're on the bottom."

Most German business firms are efficient and well run. The exceptions tend to be third- or fourth-generation, medium-

57

sized, closely held, family-owned businesses; some of these have failed to keep up with the times. Poor management can be camouflaged effectively because of organizational compartmentalization, respect for privacy, and the complete secrecy with which business is often conducted. Sometimes it isn't until bankers have been called on to bail them out that word gets around that the company is in trouble.

The extreme compartmentalization in German business creates many problems. Information flow is minimal, and quite often developments of great significance are known to only a few people. One American manager in Germany said:

> Germans not only insist on having their own space at work, but they clearly mark their territory within the organization. They will brook no interference either. This means extreme compartmentalization pervades their organization. They simply do not share information or communicate details about their divisions' operations to people outside their own area.

We have heard many stories from Germans about how difficult it is to transmit information to the decision makers; one executive said, "It is impossible to get the decision makers to listen." Compartmentalization also prevents some Germans from seeing the connection between their decisions and the results of those decisions. And while Germans often do work together on projects, the team spirit touted in many American businesses is often absent in German firms.

The cost to German business of this extreme compartmentalization is incalculable. For example, we know of one German company that takes justifiable pride in its well-made products. But quality products alone are not enough in the highly competitive world market, and unless the quality of this company's service improves to match the goods, it will continue to lose market share. Any number of people within the company have tried to make this point to top management but to no avail. The sales representatives who hear complaints from customers about poor service cannot get their message through to the people who could change the situation. There are too many German businesses which have yet to learn how to overcome this deeply imbedded compartmentalization, which is highly resistant to change.

Within each of the numerous compartments in German business, the highest-ranking person has considerable freedom and authority. What results has been described as "a hierarchy of despots." This is why it is vital to have good people at the top of each separate department in a German company.

Americans and other foreign executives complain about the lack of flexibility in German business, especially at the upper levels. Adaptability to change is hampered by, among other things, lack of management expertise. Top German executives have traditionally been technical experts. Approximately 60 percent of German manufacturing companies are headed by engineers with Ph.D.s; therefore, the German CEO probably learned management skills on the job without any formal management training.

In German business, each unit is responsible for its own performance. As in American business, goals are usually determined from above. In Germany, however, the unit is held responsible for getting the job done. Individual Germans do not generally complain; they do their best and neither ask for help nor share information.

In Germany, decision making by consensus is the rule at the working level within departments and requires much more time than the top-down decision making common in the United States. German businesses do well at planning for the long term, which has, of course, distinct advantages, but the flexibility and quick reactions necessary to deal with certain kinds of immediate problems are often absent in German business bureaucracies. In many German firms it is almost impossible to get information quickly to the people who need it; the decision-making process adds to the delay.

The German domestic market is a fraction of the size of the American market and is segmented to some extent by class as well as by region. Markets are more competitive than in the

United States. In one industry where there are twenty competitors in the U.S., there are sixty in Germany. Perhaps this is why German business executives have a reputation for "playing hardball." If they don't, they do not survive. Many companies are closely held and none are subject to the kind of government regulation or public disclosure that is found in the U.S. Public disclosure of a German company's financial condition is unheard of (compartmentalization and respect for privacy again).

German Management: Authority and Control

Germans are too busy managing to think creatively.

—French company president

In American business, the board of directors picks the CEO, sometimes following the recommendation of the departing CEO. The American CEO has full responsibility for the success of the enterprise and picks her or his own team which reports directly to the CEO. In Germany most businesses are run by two types of boards, a supervisory board (*Aufsichtsrat*) and a management board (*Vorstand*). The management board conducts the day-to-day business and monitors the firm's operations. The supervisory board approves major decisions and appoints and dismisses the management board.

During our research, it came as a surprise to learn that German middle management has little understanding of the structural relationships that make the entire organization work. Unlike the French, Germans are not articulate about the subtleties of organizational structure. Again, this ignorance may be due to the ever present compartmentalization.

The German management system is deliberately designed to be confusing. It is common practice for German business to employ at least two and sometimes three lines of authority and control:

1. There will always be a technical line of authority that follows the defined chain of command.

2. Parallel to this, one frequently finds an informal line to the top. There may be a problem discovering which of these first two lines takes precedence, a problem to be expected since the system is designed to confuse. Ambiguity has been built in as a mechanism for maintaining control; in fact it is not uncommon for the real line of authority and power to remain hidden for years and be revealed only when there is a crisis.

3. Some business firms employ the matrix system of organization, which can be likened to a grid, with organizational authority running through normal channels directly to the top and substantive lines of authority running down and then laterally to all compartments on a particular level.

German lines of authority must be followed religiously. Key people must be informed about all developments, and any major decision involving new projects or significant amounts of money must go to the top for approval. Usually, there are two or three officials in a medium or large company whose approval is required for these decisions, and naturally that creates bottlenecks.

As we noted earlier, within departments, at the working level, consensus is the goal in reaching decisions. Thus, decision making frequently takes longer than in the United States. On the other hand, the implementation time is much shorter. This is one more example of how German business is more thorough, more conservative, and more cautious than its American counterpart. The practice of requiring lateral clearances takes time, but Germans are working in a much longer time frame than Americans.

At the *Vorstand* level, executives in charge of finance, production, marketing, sales, etc., have direct lines of influence to all parts of the organization.

Some German business firms follow the American organizational pattern because of the influence of executives trained in

American business schools as well as the influence of American management consultants. Integrating the management practices of two cultures is extremely difficult and requires great wisdom, flexibility, and tact.

German managers are expected to solve their own departmental problems. They don't make waves and they don't present problems to others for resolution. American executives in Germany have to learn not to look over the shoulders of their German workers. German managers expect a great deal of their subordinates and test them by pushing them to perform, but they do not hover.

Because changes in procedures are resisted in Germany, American managers who feel that they must put their individual stamp on the job and initiate changes can create serious problems. To the Germans, the only way a work force can be "perfect" is if its procedures are spelled out *and remain constant*. As one might imagine, changes by German management are much less frequent than by American management.

Certain American management practices are especially disruptive to a German office. One of these is the last-minute request for overtime. German employees are protected by many government regulations covering coffee breaks and overtime. Such time regulations are rigorously enforced and American management cannot expect German secretaries or clerks to give up their coffee breaks or work overtime unless it is arranged well in advance.

Employee Expectations

An important component of German character is the high value placed on hard work, especially among top executives (managers often work fifty hours a week). This dedication has become increasingly crucial as the incentive to work hard at middle and lower levels has weakened somewhat, in part because of the fact that it is now almost impossible to fire an employee in Germany. Supervisors in German business must motivate subordinates and elicit their cooperation and support (which does not mean hovering, which will be resented).

To motivate German employees, we suggest that you find someone to coach you in the finer points of relating to a German staff. There will be very different expectations and hidden obstacles. For example, in the United States, when employees need to be criticized, good managers usually begin by complimenting employees on something they have done well before telling them what change or improvement is needed. Germans won't understand this sort of communication; in fact, they will be made quite anxious by the ambiguity of a compliment joined with a criticism and will wonder what is really being said. One very successful Japanese executive had this to say:

> I have many German employees and I must make a periodic evaluation of their performance. Then I must meet with each employee and discuss his evaluation. Sometimes the German will say, "Why did you give me only an average rating?" I tell him, "You come in late and you are not working hard." He will say, "But why didn't you tell me this before?"
>
> Now I write a letter to any employee who arrives late all the time and I also give him detailed comments on his work if it is less than satisfactory. Germans pay attention to written communications.

As this example shows, it is absolutely necessary to communicate directly and frankly with German employees. It is also best to do so in private, to remain low-key about your feelings and clear about what you expect. If a German employee is not performing well, a superior must tell the employee so or be considered negligent.

The Japanese executive makes the important point of putting comments in writing. If the verbal message does not produce the desired improvement in performance, a written communication is necessary. This provides an official record of the superior's evaluation to be used later if the need arises. As the Japanese executive says: "I advise foreign managers to learn to express their thoughts clearly and in detail and to put them in writing. Otherwise they will never reach German employees." Also, since Germans are very print-oriented, foreign managers must hone their writing skills.

It should come as no surprise that Germans are perfectionists. They automatically expect perfection in themselves and in others. They rarely compliment someone on a job well done because they take it for granted that people will perform well. However, they do bend over backwards to be fair. Generally, German workers will expect that:

1. procedures will be orderly and followed faithfully,

2. presentations will consist of a logical exposition of ideas,

3. detailed information will be provided about everything involved,

4. privacy and personal space will be safe from intrusion,

5. the correct German rules for personal behavior will be followed,

6. formality and politeness, including proper respect for social and business status, will pervade daily business life,

7. power, money, and influence will not be displayed ostentatiously,

8. frankness, honesty, and directness will govern human relations.

Business Etiquette

Germans greet each other in the office (and everywhere else) formally with *"Guten Tag"* and a handshake. In fact as much as twenty minutes every day may be devoted to shaking hands, which occurs at the beginning of the day and again at the end. Americans should not lose sight of the importance of this gesture of respect and courtesy.

German white-collar employees are very conscious of their rights and status and must be handled with respect. Never give a direct order to a fellow employee who is your equal in office rank, and never talk down to anyone. German employees on the whole are better trained and better educated than are Americans. A German university degree means more than its American equivalent because the German educational system is more rigorous, and a smaller percentage of the population gains college entrance. A German undergraduate degree is on a par with a master's degree from an American university. Likewise, German business executives are well versed in history, philosophy, literature, geography, music, and art. It is taken for granted that the women and men who work in business offices as secretaries, assistants, and junior management personnel are well educated, able to speak a foreign language, and capable of producing coherent, intelligible, thoughtful communications. You can expect that a well-placed German executive secretary (who often has a university degree) will be able to draft correspondence if you simply describe the basic content and desired tone of your message. In general secretaries expect to have more responsibility than is customary in the United States, and they are to be treated as professionals and addressed by an honorific and last name: "Frau (or Herr) Schmidt." We have heard many stories of the damage done by American executives calling their German secretaries by their first names, which is overly familiar and condescending in the context of German culture.

During business dinners there are certain ceremonies to be observed. You will notice that Germans offer very formal toasts, raising their glasses and looking directly into the eyes of the person being toasted. They sit erect and their gestures are precise. In Germany, toasting is a ceremony to be taken seriously and executed correctly. You will need coaching and practice to do it. It is part of correct business behavior.

Labor: Bottom-Up Power

One of the greatest assets of German business is its system of apprenticeship training. Young German workers spend two or more years learning their jobs. During this period they work

65

three days a week and spend two or three days in school. Since their education is reinforced by hands-on job experience, they form a well-qualified work force. The importance of this apprenticeship training to overall performance has received too little recognition and is often overlooked by American economists.

The labor movement in Germany, from the shop to the boardroom (where labor is represented) is very powerful, and German labor relations are substantially different from those in the United States. For example, any deviations from established patterns of work schedules require approval of the *Betriebsrat* (works council). The works council has authority over personnel and must approve all personnel transfers, even those within a department. An American executive must either learn to deal with the works council directly, which can take an inordinate amount of time and may prove impossible, or must rely on a highly skilled local colleague.

The power of the works council results in greater job security for the German worker than is found in the United States. Working conditions and wages are generally among the highest in the world. German laws also make it difficult to fire employees; instead, German firms often simply bypass incompetent employees for promotion or put them in niches where they can do the least damage. To avoid too much deadwood, one of the most valued skills that a manager in Germany can develop is that of being able to motivate employees and elicit the best possible performance. Fortunately, "doing things right" is still a core value throughout German society.

There is a relatively narrow salary spread between top management and lower echelons, which is radically different from pay scales in the United States. This more equitable pay scale helps maintain a high level of employee morale, as does the generous package of fringe benefits most German workers receive: complete health coverage, life insurance, social security, child-care assistance, six or more weeks' vacation, an annual bonus of one month's salary, and an optional bonus for high performance. This additional bonus constitutes virtually the only leverage top management has over middle management and middle management over subordinates.

Germans are not as mobile in their careers as their American counterparts. They do not change jobs often. German businesses value loyalty, a sense of duty, and obedience in their employees. By and large, most Germans stay with a firm for years, if not for life.

Compared to Americans, Germans at all levels have much more job security—especially during recessions, when many capable, hardworking Americans are likely to be unemployed. In an article for *Stern,* Eva Windmoller compared working life in Germany with life in the U.S.:

> Most of the Americans we know could only dream of a living standard as high as the Germans. Americans work harder, earn less, are entitled to fourteen days of paid leave per year, three weeks at the *very* most, have very few fringe benefits in the way of pension funds and medical insurance. The competition's greater, stress is higher. After all, the boss can fire them tomorrow, and the employee will get a few weeks' pay if his employer's generous; they're entitled to twenty-six weeks of unemployment pay, somewhere between $25 and $125 per week, and that's it.

Women in German Business

German women have less status in the business world than American women. Few married German women work outside the home, and the percentage of German women in professions and business is far lower than in the United States. This is particularly true at the managerial level; only 16 percent of German executives are female.

Therefore, we give a special word of warning to American women who plan to work in Germany: don't expect attitudes towards women to be the same as they are in the United States. As a businesswoman you will not only have to prove yourself, but you will be regarded with wariness, even more so than in the United States. You may also encounter some resentment on the part of female employees as well as from male colleagues.

Making friends and running a household present special challenges for working women. Since German stores are not open in the evening or weekends (except for Saturday morning), shopping for food, clothing, and household items is difficult. Social life is limited for foreigners unless they already have German friends, and the isolation and loneliness can be painful. We were able to interview only three American women working for German companies at the managerial level, and each said she missed the contact, support, and encouragement of other women that she had experienced in the United States. Even German career women find it hard to make friends. One German editor who had worked for seven years in the United States returned to Germany and felt isolated and unhappy for the first year because she missed the social life she had found in New York.

Negotiations: Power in Action

The first barrier in any intercultural negotiation is language. Unless your German counterparts speak English or you are fluent in German, you will need a first-rate, well-educated interpreter whom you have briefed in great detail. Even if you speak German well, be aware that Germans often use an elevated form of the language in business dealings, a form that may not be readily understood by nonnatives.

In negotiations, as in most things, the German approach is slow, logical, and analytical. Your own presentation should therefore be logical and low-key, with no hype, dramatics, or unsupported claims. Voice and speech are important: be sure your voice is firm and controlled and your speech well modulated. Speak slowly. The leader of the German team will project his authority in a forceful tone, and so any hesitancy on your part will signal weakness. Be self-controlled at all times; keep a poker face; do not fidget; and never reveal impatience.

During negotiations Germans keep their distance. They appear sober and earnest, especially the senior management

68

personnel, who are usually more formal and reserved than younger German managers.

Germans play hardball and are determined to get the best possible deal. Stubborn and persistent, they will press for price advantage and for every concession they want. "To work with Germans you need good nerves," according to one veteran French negotiator.

Reaching an agreement takes time; be patient. There will be long delays between the end of negotiations and final acceptance by the Vorstand, so don't be deceived into thinking the Germans have lost interest or are stalling. The final agreement will be delivered in writing, often on preprinted standard forms.

Getting Started

Two absolutely essential ingredients in starting a business in Germany are a first-rate German lawyer and well-placed bankers. Any American firm would be well advised to spend time researching the resources in these two fields and seeking the advice and counsel of both American and German business executives in Germany. You may already have good attorneys and bankers in the United States, but that does not necessarily mean they have the contacts you need in Germany. In Germany, bankers provide a proportionally greater share of business financing than they do in the U.S. and are close allies of their business clients. European bankers in general are much more involved with their business clients on a day-to-day basis and have close connections with government as well, in order to keep abreast of changing regulations.

Some American firms, since they are not familiar with the multiple roles of European bankers, fail to make full use of the services German banks offer. European bankers provide more than just financial advice and assistance. They have vital information about your industry and can arrange the necessary introductions to important contacts. Both German banks and international banks operating in Germany have experts who can assist you, for instance, in dealing with the government and with governmental regulations. This can be valuable help since the German government is actively involved in every phase of business life and one must deal with a maze of bureaucracies. The right kind of German banker can also refer you to reliable executive placement firms for recruiting competent managers and other key personnel. The time spent talking to various bankers and assessing their ability to work with you and your company is time well spent and should be a top priority.

Government regulations for employees are more stringent and more strictly enforced than in the United States. Regulations govern not only how many hours employees can work, but also such things as holidays, bonuses, the space that must be allotted each worker, and the proximity of the worker to windows for daylight.

The government also regulates shopping hours. German stores close at 6:00 P.M. during the week and at midday on Saturday, except for one Saturday per month. This is to comply with union demands for shorter hours and also to protect the proprietors of small stores with few employees. By closing all stores early, small store owners have enough time off and will not be in an unfair competitive position with big stores (who have enough employees to remain open longer). This may be fair to the small store owner, but it is dreadfully inconvenient for all working people who need weekend and evening shopping hours. Such limited shopping hours have a great influence on the kind of advertising found in Germany, as we shall see.

As you would expect, it takes much longer to establish a business on firm footing in Germany than it does in the United States. This is because it is necessary first to earn a good reputation and to develop the proper relationships with distributors, dealers, and retailers, all of whom play roles far more strategic than the average American executive expects. German distributors and salespeople must know their customers; since Germans prefer long-term relationships in both personal and business life, they need to know and feel secure about the people upon whom they depend. The German executive's credibility is on the line when a product gets to the marketplace.

Salespeople spend years cultivating clients and building a reputation for reliability. Naturally, they want clients to be satisfied. Also, it should be noted that German salespeople are usually better informed about their products than are most American salespeople.

Given the great differences between German and American business, it is clear that the wise American manager learns how to survive and prosper in the German market, with a German work force, German distributors, German advertising, German lawyers, and German bankers.

Advertising: Facts and More Facts

Each nation and each culture have their own ways of describing their products and the company behind the products. These stylistic variations evolve through a natural process of interaction between advertisers, media, and the marketplace.

German ads are loaded with detailed information; products are described and analyzed. Often, even in the national media, ads tell precisely where the product can be bought and at what price. German products sell because the quality is good and the price is competitive, not because of an attractive image. Germans appear to be unbelievably low-context in almost everything having to do with advertising. Ads are examined and picked apart—not just by the government (which monitors advertising) but by readers as well. Furthermore, readers write companies to complain if they dislike an ad.

Given the limited hours stores are open, it is very difficult for customers to do much comparison shopping. They simply do not have the time; instead, they depend upon the advertiser to provide them with the detailed information on which to base comparisons and make choices.

Good advertising strategies in Germany take into account that Germans are both print-oriented and very literal-minded. Since television advertising is strictly limited and tightly controlled (including content) by the government, a much greater proportion of a company's advertising budget will focus on print media. And, as detailed above, the print ads convey information rather than evoke a mood or appeal to subliminal emotions and desires. One Japanese manufacturer of office machines experimented with an ad showing a pretty woman standing next to one of the company's machines. The German response was one of confusion: "What is that woman doing there? What purpose does she serve?"

A French manufacturer of automotive accessories kept urging the German managing director of its subsidiary in Germany to advertise their product on German television. The German manager resisted for two reasons: he knew the target audience watched little television and the product was new in Germany. He suggested print ads instead. Finally, he gave in to the constant pressure from the Paris home office, but he decided to run a controlled test by advertising in four different media—television, radio, billboards, and print ads—simultaneously. The print ads were far and away the most effective. Why? Print ads permitted the company to describe in great detail the many features of the new product and to back up the description with the almost encyclopedic details that appeal to German consumers, who would otherwise have been skeptical because of its newness.

Several executives told us that the two biggest problems for advertisers in Germany are government regulations and competitor complaints. The government forbids any kind of comparative advertising; you cannot claim your product is the best or that it is better than a competitor's. Ads are policed, and if there is a legitimate complaint made against your ad, it must be withdrawn, which means you may not use it in any form. You may also face a lawsuit. Further, the government restricts the use of celebrities in ads; you must be able to prove that the celebrity actually uses the product. Our best advice is to have your attorney check all ads before publication.

Sometimes when an agency prepares a very attractive ad, a competitor will claim ownership of the text and charge the first company with a violation of copyright laws. Copyright claims often rest on fine points of interpretation in the law and can lead to lengthy legal battles. Again, consult your attorney.

Another serious problem, which Germans share with Americans, occurs when German employees move from one advertising agency to another. Clients often do not want to reveal future campaign plans or give confidential information to an agency for fear the information will be given to competitors when employees change jobs. Obviously, such a fear handicaps agencies in preparing campaigns for new products.

Germans are bewildered by the size and style of American business, especially in the advertising world. The constant changes, the lack of continuity, the hyperbole and flamboyance—all puzzle and annoy them. In Germany things stay in place for years. One German advertising man complained about his experience in the U.S., where he was working for a large agency. He not only was assigned the accounts for two major competing food companies in the same year, but he had to deal with new brand managers every two or three months. Furthermore, each brand manager wanted to put his stamp on the account and as a consequence changed everything that had been done by his predecessor. Is it any wonder there was no continuity?

Health is an important theme in German advertising, especially for cosmetics, toilet articles, and food. The appearance of being healthy is very important to Germans, whether it is manifested in intangibles such as proper eating habits or in a glowing skin, rosy cheeks, a suntan, and shining hair.

The success of pattern advertising (using the same slogan or brand name in every country) is another difference between the U.S. and German advertising styles. A German executive made the following comment: "Lots of American firms want to use pattern advertising. If you're Coca-Cola, pattern advertising works. But if you're not, all you do is remind people that you're not German." In other words, pattern advertising will only be effective in Germany if the product is already as well known as Coca-Cola.

The rigid regulations that govern life in Germany are evident in the advertising world as well, as the following story, told by a foreign managing director of an advertising agency in Germany, illustrates:

> The managing director signed a contract for 1000 promotional flyers, to cost 1000 DMs. When the order was delivered, there were 1100 flyers and a bill for 1100 DMs. When the client asked about the 100 extra flyers and 100 extra DMs, the printer replied, "It's the German way." The client's home office refused to pay the bill. The managing director called his German attorney, who told him that they would have to pay because by law the printer is allowed ten percent overage on all orders. Thereafter, the managing director told the printer the amount of money budgeted for each order, and requested that the printer figure in his overage to keep the total at the specified level.

When you are presenting a new product in the German market it must be described in detail so that Germans will understand exactly where it fits into the market. In the words of one German advertising executive, "This is especially important if you are adding to your line or if you want to upgrade it. Always target your buyer and appeal to his intelligence and taste. Stress quality and service."

As incredible as it may sound to Americans, the time allocated to commercials on German television is limited to a total of twenty minutes per day. The American home office often responds to this information by telling its German subsidiary, "Buy all twenty minutes!" But, it may take years to get any of that time. First priority is given to companies that advertised the year before. Whatever time these companies do not buy is the only time available to new accounts. An advertising agency cannot buy time, only an advertiser. If an advertiser then decides not to use the time it has purchased, it may cancel but cannot sell the time to another company.

In a German company, the advertising director, possibly in consultation with the marketing director, makes the decisions

74

and is responsible for advertising. Advertising decisions are not made by the chief executive, as they often are in the United States. One of our German respondents, the head of a large subsidiary of a well-known American firm, provided us with a number of particularly insightful comments on this subject:

> Advertising in the States centers around the chief executive—the man at the top. In Germany, the man at the top is usually not interested in advertising because this responsibility is delegated to the director of marketing [three or four notches below him in the company]. Advertising is subordinate to marketing, which also includes pricing, packaging, promotion and distribution.
>
> Americans make a big mistake because they're always talking about how this campaign is the biggest, greatest, or newest. It's the same as last year's campaign, only they're talking about it as if it were entirely new. The Germans really get tired of what you call "hype." Americans come with ten people and they want to see the president. They ignore the man who is responsible and go to the "man at the top." The head man simply tells them, "You'll have to see Herr So-and-So, director of marketing, and Herr Y, who is the advertising director." Of course, the Americans by then have made an enemy of the advertising director by going over his head. Yet he's the man they're going to have to work with.
>
> It seems Americans always want us to do things their way. But it doesn't work that way in Germany. The Association of Packagers had a convention in San Francisco. They had dancing girls and everything. Now they want us to have the same thing here. In Germany conventions are serious, tough, and boring. It's strictly business. The dancing girls give us the wrong image.

This is a good example of releasing the wrong response.

Americans from the German Perspective

Viewed from the German perspective, Americans are rich in resources but lacking in a number of desirable character traits. Germans often describe Americans as being overly familiar, intrusive, historically and politically naive, poorly educated, narrow in viewpoint, undisciplined, lacking in taste, profligate, unmindful of the proper care of property, vacillating in decision making, shallow, boastful, and overly self-confident. They think American business associates require an inordinate amount of attention and direction and need constant evaluation and "hand-holding."

On the positive side, Germans often see Americans as friendly, open, resourceful, energetic, innovative, and, in general, capable in business (but with an uneven track record). Germans who know Americans well admit that Americans have greater freedom, are generally happier, and are more productive and more creative than many other people. They think American society has great resilience with an unusual capacity to "bounce back" from difficult times. They recognize that no other country in the world offers more opportunities to succeed, and in no other country have so many people risen from the bottom to the top in a single generation.

Germans from the American Perspective

Some of the terms used most frequently by Americans to describe Germans include highly disciplined, well educated, neat and orderly. They also speak of the Germans as systematic, well organized, meticulous about appointments and deadlines, and efficient in their work. Many Americans also consider them perfectionists. Some Americans find them hard to get to know— not unfriendly, but reserved. In business Germans are described as oriented toward procedures but bending over backwards to be fair; they also note that Germans are secretive and do not share information. Most Americans agree that Germans play hardball and are tough competitors. Away from business, they are very protective of their privacy.

On the negative side, some Americans complain that Germans are pushy in service lines (at the market or at the airport), noisy in bars and restaurants, and often insensitive to the feelings of others. Americans with a speaking knowledge of German find it easier to make friends with Germans than those without the language, of course. Most Americans we talked to agreed that it takes a long time to make good German friends but they all said it was worth the effort, and many Americans in the U.S. commented on how much they missed their German friends.

Advice To Americans Doing Business In Germany

What follows summarizes the most crucial points about doing business in Germany and includes recommendations deemed essential by executives who have been successful there. This does not mean that there aren't exceptions to this advice; however, it has been our experience that executives who don't think the rules apply to them are the ones most likely to become submerged in a morass of inexplicable complications in a foreign country.

1. *Choose your foreign representatives with care.*

While there are hundreds of things one needs to know to work in any country, most fall in the sphere of certain kinds of experts, such as bankers, lawyers, accountants, and economists. American business executives operating in the United States depend on these experts and usually have a coterie either on retainer or as part of the company staff. While your company's attorneys or accountants may be the best in their specialties in the United States, they are not necessarily knowledgeable outside their specialties or outside the country. When your American attorney, banker, or accountant recommends a foreign representative, satisfy yourself that this person is the best available for your needs in Germany. You will want someone who can mobilize local experts with demonstrated skills in your particular business. Although most German business executives speak English, fluency in English is much less important than a person's intelligence, education, experience, and business connections. You especially need to find out if a candidate operates from a position of power and influence—at least enough to be of value to you. In choosing a foreign representative, consult a knowledgeable, experienced German "headhunter" in a top executive placement firm, which your German banker can recommend.

2. Integrate your foreign operations.

Synchronize the introduction of new products so they appear in the American and German markets simultaneously. Germans are neither stupid nor uninformed. In a fast-moving field (such as cosmetics, for instance) any delay in the German market simply gives your competitors an advantage and tips your hand. It's a small thing, but failure to observe this rule can result in substantial losses by your foreign subsidiary. There is nothing a German manager can do to rectify a mistake in timing made by your home office.

3. Avoid the "now you are going to do it our way" approach.

There are many ways of reaching an overseas market. Starting from scratch is usually rejected in favor of buying a company that already has a foothold in the marketplace. Since American managers almost inevitably assert themselves by putting their stamp on the business, it is necessary to keep a tight rein on American managers working in Germany until they have been in place long enough to really know why things are done the way they are.

The American businesses that have done well in Germany have bought small subsidiaries and made changes slowly. By moving only when they had a good feeling for the possible consequences, they helped insure their future success. We know that for Americans there is always an urge to get things going in a big way. But that's not the way it's done in Germany. Keep in mind that whatever Germans do, there is a reason for it.

One German executive tells his American clients, "You don't have to do it the way they do, but find out why they do it that way and really understand it." Don't change a policy until you are sure that the reasoning behind it no longer applies. Also remember that because the German market is relatively small and

78

intimate, everyone will know what you are doing. You must give them time to get used to your presence.

4. *Educate yourself about business conditions.*

Know your competition, know your market, know your legal and financial status, know your media, and know your labor force. Virtually any changes you may want to make in personnel—even within the same office—can be costly if not handled properly. Find someone who has had experience and who knows how to deal with labor—then take that person's advice. Business in Germany is tough. In some industries your competitors will number three times what they do in the United States. The market is tiny compared to what it is in the States and competition is fierce. German laws are often repressive, more strictly enforced, and there are more of them.

5. *Build personal relationships.*

People are your most valuable asset. Since people produce, distribute, sell, and make up the working core of your organization—and are also your customers—there is nothing more important than reaching people. This means motivating them, inspiring them, directing them, providing them with opportunities, and making friends with them. No organization can survive without the active participation and help of the people who staff it. In Germany the company employees are like close cousins—members of the same family—but with different experiences and histories. You need to get to know them. It's important to remember that if an American wants to motivate or get cooperation from Germans, it must be done in terms of German behavior. German expectations about everything from daily formalities like greetings and handshakes to basic management practices must be observed. Although some things are obviously more important than others, none can be considered trivial.

Also, note that when it comes to dealing with American companies, Germans prefer to deal with one person; they do not like to be shunted around or forced to deal with committees.

6. *Supervise, but don't hover.*

In any business there has to be a balance between control and freedom in order to get on with the work. No American would dream of telling a master machinist how to set up the lathe for a particular piece of work on a production line. If the manager did, it would demonstrate that (a) the manager didn't know anything about managing and (b) the manager was ignorant of the machinists' subculture. Whether we like it or not, Americans are notorious all over the world for looking over people's shoulders and telling them how to do things. A vital piece of advice for handling the Germans is to treat all of them with the same respect and care with which you would treat any competent professional. Remember that one reason German managers tend to keep their doors closed is to avoid the appearance of intruding on their employees.

The general rules for Americans in Germany are: less supervision, fewer reports, fewer financial controls, and more delegation. Spend the necessary staff time meeting and reaching consensus and then, "hands off."

7. *Budget for additional staff to prepare financial reports.*

Feeling a need for constant evaluation, American business has adopted the practice of requiring detailed financial reports from all subordinate units. American companies have adapted to this practice and are geared to provide the necessary detailed financial information quarterly or even monthly. By contrast, German business works on an annual schedule with reports required only once a year. As a consequence, German businesses are not set up to provide the kind of detailed quarterly financial information Americans often expect. According to our banking sources, many German businesses and subsidiaries have been driven into a state of chaos by American demands for quarterly financial reports, with the result that important business matters are neglected.

As one German executive put it, "These American reporting requirements can literally drive a company into the ground . . .

destroying people's rhythms and the order of the office." Since the American banks and insurance companies providing the financing for American companies will insist on quarterly financial reports, American companies with German subsidiaries should budget for additional staff to prepare these quarterly reports and to take into account the organizational adjustments that have to be made. These adjustments will take time.

8. Establish a policy for learning the language and culture.

A basic rule for working in any foreign country which is particularly applicable to Germany is "learn the language, learn the language, learn the language." Don't send people who are not willing to study the language, and make sure assignments are long enough (a minimum of five years) to be worth the effort. Bear the cost and reward employees for learning the language. Americans in Germany can't evaluate performance accurately without knowing the language, nor can they negotiate or make friends who can be trusted and who can help interpret German culture and behavior.

Because we are all preoccupied with controlling our own input, Americans tend to be attracted to those Germans who speak the best English. This gives skilled English-speaking Germans a tremendous advantage over Germans who are less fluent. One of the best arguments for American managers learning the local language is that they will have a better basis for evaluating performance. Right now Americans have a reputation for promoting Germans who speak good English over those who are better performers. There is no need to elaborate on the effect of this on morale and performance.

9. Allow more time in meetings for individual agendas.

In German meetings everyone has an agenda. Provide an opportunity for all these agendas to be considered, even if it takes more time than you would like. Germans are used to long meetings and their communication style demands that they provide a lot of background, history, and an inordinate amount of detail.

10. *Develop effective procedures. Here are some basic rules for keeping Germans satisfied:*

Answer all correspondence within one week, preferably, the next day.

Answer all questions raised in correspondence.

Submit all reports on time, and supply information even when it seems unnecessary or trivial.

Be particularly careful to meet all time commitments: deliveries, deadlines, production schedules.

If you schedule a meeting, have an agenda prepared in advance and complete all arrangements before the Germans arrive.

11. *Give your advertising a German flavor.*

In Germany it is particularly important to project a German image. Not only are the Germans slow to change their buying habits, but they also have a very strong identification with their own products, which they know are well made, well designed and created to last. Unfortunately, not all American goods have a strong reputation in the German marketplace.

American advertising is directed toward creating new, trendy images. Germans are not impressed with novelty. They want quality, performance, durability and, most of all, *information, not hype.* Whether your advertising agency is international or local, the input should come from experts on German advertising. American account executives should not expect to discuss advertising with the president of a German company.

12. *Be conservative in everything you do.*

Dress conservatively, on and off the job. Avoid anything that draws attention to yourself including conversational taboos. Politically, Germany is much more polarized than is the United States. There are deep cleavages between left and right, and it is assumed that one's political philosophy underpins everything one does. Also, politics is a more important factor in everyday life in Germany than it is in the United States. It is best to avoid political discussions and the expression of political opinions. Be familiar with the major political parties, but don't get involved— and be sure to keep strong opinions to yourself. The old rule that one never discusses politics, religion, or money still applies.

Americans Working for Germans

Not all Americans who work for Germans are actually in Germany; many are in the United States working in German-owned subsidiaries or joint ventures, often with German bosses. The following account illustrates the kind of cross-cultural encounter Americans may experience:

Tom Wright had his first appointment with his new manager, Herr Bruning from Düsseldorf. Arriving three minutes after the appointed hour, he knocked on Bruning's office door. Bruning opened the door and looked directly at Wright with a stern and unsmiling expression, and after a vigorous handshake motioned Wright to a chair. Bruning then launched into a detailed list of information he required immediately. Wright was taken aback by Bruning's brusqueness and, in an effort the bridge the distance between them, moved his chair forward a few inches, which seemed to annoy Bruning. As soon as Bruning finished reading his list, he said, "I will need that information by 2:00 P.M. today." He then rose, indicating the interview was over. Still seeking a way to create a friendlier atmosphere, Wright asked how Bruning's family was adjusting to their new American home. Bruning looked surprised and replied curtly, "Everything is normal," then motioned Wright toward the door.

Wright left the interview wondering where he had gone wrong. He hadn't expected such a short meeting with a long list of business questions to be answered immediately; rather, he anticipated an exploratory session for the two men to get acquainted and for Bruning to brief him as second-in-command on the new ground rules and management style. Wright was convinced that he had somehow offended Bruning and that Bruning did not like him.

How can we interpret this encounter? What misunderstandings and misperceptions have occurred? First, Wright was a few minutes late; Germans value promptness and find tardiness, especially from a subordinate, intolerable. Wright misinterpreted Bruning's brusque manner and immediate plunge into business as signs of irritation or hostility; he didn't understand that Germans are very direct and get right down to business with a minimum of pleasantries. When Wright moved his chair closer to his boss's desk, Bruning was indeed offended. Germans do not adjust the furniture in someone else's office, and since German social and business interaction distance is greater than American, Wright was in effect invading Bruning's personal territory. Bruning also considered Wright's question about his family too personal and unsuitable for a business relationship.

PART 3

The French

When we refer to the French, we mean the people of northern France, especially those who live and work in Paris and Lyon, where many major business firms are headquartered. This is where we conducted our interviews with French women and men in business and the professions.

FRENCH CULTURE

Historical Background: Context for Today

The French long to be unified and pacified, by force if necessary, led to harmony, saved from ruin, and made prosperous by one man, a man who can enforce law and order, bridge the gap between mediocre reality and their national dream.

—Luigi Barzini, *The Europeans*

Rene de Chateaubriand once said that "the French are attracted by power." Their heroes are the people who have led the nation to greatness from the time of Clovis, the king of the Franks: Hugh Capet, Philippe August, Saint Louis, Henry IV, Louis XIV, Jeanne d'Arc, Jean Baptiste Colbert, Napoleon, and, in modern times, Charles de Gaulle. During their lifetime these leaders may have provoked anger and dissension, but, in retrospect, they are revered because of their powerful leadership and their ability to unify France.

The importance of French history to the average French person can hardly be overstated. The French live surrounded by thousands of monuments to their glorious past. Every quarter in Paris has its historically important statues, buildings or fountains, daily reminders of past achievements. French villages have statues to local heroes and important political leaders. As a result of this constant immersion in history, the French tend to see things in their historical context and relate contemporary events to their origins.

In the days of the monarchy, the church was powerful because there was a close association between church and state. Since the French Revolution, the church has lost its position of influence and power; today, religion is no longer the unified political force it once was in French society. Eighty-five percent of the population is nominally Catholic, but most people only attend church for ceremonial occasions: baptisms, marriages, and funerals. The French Catholic church today is split into many factions and has become quite politicized. Nevertheless, Ca-

87

tholicism is still a strong element in French culture on the informal level, similar to Protestantism (especially the work ethic) in German and American cultures.

Regionalism: Geographic and Ethnic Diversity

There are many regional differences in France and several distinct subcultures, each with its own character and personality. One can still find evidence of the influence of the English in Normandy, the Germans in Alsace-Lorraine, the Italians in Provence, the Celts in Bretagne, and the Spanish in the Pyrenees. However, the dominant theme in France, which countervails the divisiveness of regional blocs, is the common heritage of *nos ancêtres les Gaulois*.

France is where north and south meet, and over the years France has absorbed, albeit gradually, hundreds of thousands of people from North Africa and the other Mediterranean countries. The recent influx of foreigners is causing severe social problems, exacerbated by an economic recession and unemployment.

The various subcultures within France have had an impact on the society, and the Mediterranean subcultures have given France an additional Latin flavor. For a more detailed description of the impact of immigration on France, the reader is referred to a brilliant and witty book *The French,* by Theodor Zeldin; we also urge readers to consult Flora Lewis's *Europe,* which has a splendid chapter on France that gives in-depth historical background in a highly readable style (see reading list).

French Time: Doing Many Things at Once

The most important thing to know about the French is that they are high on the polychronic scale. This means they do many things at once; they can tolerate constant interruptions and are totally involved with people; they maintain direct eye contact and use all their senses: visual, auditory, and olfactory. They love to talk and communicate with their whole body as well as with the spoken language. Their faces are very expressive as are their gestures, all of which reflect the intensity of their involvement with each other.

As a result of this involvement, French perception and handling of time is very different from the German or American system. Because they are highly polychronic, the French don't always adhere to schedules or appointments, delivery dates, or deadlines. It's wise to reconfirm appointments one or two days in advance, and don't be alarmed if you have to wait; *c'est normal.* In a polychronic system there are apt to be many interruptions and emergencies. If the telephone rings as a Frenchman is going out the door to an appointment, he must stop and speak to the caller. Like all polychronic people, the French have elaborate information networks which include clients, friends, and family, and these networks must be maintained scrupulously if they are to function effectively. For this reason promptness is not always to be expected.

The polychronic French also think nothing of changing plans at the last minute. This is very unsettling to most Americans and Germans, who consider such behavior irresponsible. But remember that in a polychronic culture, particularly one as high-context as the French, the vast information networks provide individuals with a constant update on the changing economic or political conditions that vitally affect their business. New information may require a change in plans to accommodate to changing conditions. What may appear to be a capricious change of mind is often in reality a sensible adjustment.

Long-term planning is especially difficult for the French. They are all too aware of the many things that may prevent their keeping a commitment. Conditions may change, people may change. How can one predict the future? Many French people have difficulty planning even a month in advance; planning for a year ahead is often impossible. This is because the French expect interruptions and changes in their schedules. One Frenchman who was invited to give a speech the following year panicked; "How can I possibly know what I will be doing then?" he asked. Given this approach to planning, it is easy to see why the French often have enormous difficulty with the Germans, who routinely plan for the future in great detail.

Another factor that affects French handling of time is the importance of *savoir-vivre*. The French insist on enjoying life now, making the most of each day. This includes living with a certain style and elegance, which is far more important than being a slave to some abstract idea of deadlines or schedules. As a result, French deadlines have an elastic quality to allow for life's uncertainties.

French Tempo: *Vite, Vite*

In their body movements, the French are quick and flexible, moving with a rapid, staccato beat. They don't do things in a slow or measured way, as Germans do. They rush. Their faces communicate their reactions; they raise their eyebrows, they smile, gesture, and shrug their shoulders. Even if you cannot understand the language, you can almost decipher their message just by watching them. They smile more than Germans and their handshake is not as rigid.

In decision making, the French are able to move more rapidly than the Germans because they have a highly centralized authority structure. French executives can and do make independent decisions and don't have to go through the long, time-consuming process of lateral clearances or wade through several levels in the hierarchy for decisions, as is common in Germany.

The tempo of the business day is also different in the two countries. As one German executive described it, "The French start slowly and build; they peak at late afternoon and continue going strong far into the evening. The Germans start right out in the early morning and maintain a steady work pace with a slowdown at the end of the day. They are much more apt to have a short lunch hour and leave at 5:00 P.M."

90

French Space: Centralization

French space is a reflection of French culture and French institutions. Everything is centralized, and spatially the entire country is laid out around centers, with Paris as the most important hub.

French cities are spiders in the center of a grand web—roads radiating out, roads crossing the radials. You are the fly venturing into that force field.

—Denise McCluggage, author and race car driver

Within big cities there are many circles and centers from which the streets radiate. The Paris *metro* is a series of centers linked by different lines.

Paris has been the center of everything French for centuries: the capital and the seat of a vast government bureaucracy and the center of business, publishing, education, and the arts (contrasted to decentralized Germany, which was unified late in its history).

In recent years the French government has tried to encourage the development of regional centers and has begun to disperse government activities and to encourage business to do the same. For example, Lyon, the second largest city in France, has become a commercial center of growing importance. Many business firms, both French and foreign, now have offices in Lyon. Some executives prefer Lyon to Paris because it is much less expensive and less crowded, although it remains easily accessible thanks to excellent rail and air services. Toulouse, Bordeaux, Lille, and Grenoble are also important centers of commerce and industry. It will be interesting to see how the French respond to the decentralization programs because the need for centralization is still very strong in French culture.

French authority is also highly centralized; the person in the center of any organization or any office is the person in control. In a large French office with many people, the person in the center of the space is the boss. If a newcomer joins the office, her or his desk will usually be placed farthest from the center.

91

Centralization in social organization runs throughout the history of France. It was most pronounced during the reign of the great French kings, when the royal courts flowered. French courts were renowned for their radiating circles of power and influence. Power at court was achieved in part by birth, since those of noble blood were born with rank and status. But power was also achieved by the skillful manipulation of the courtiers who endlessly maneuvered for status around the kings and queens. Those engaged in constant jockeying for favor became highly skilled at detecting subtle signs of pleasure or displeasure reflecting the waxing or waning of influence among those close to the monarchs.

Personal Space and Regional Differences

The French stand and sit closer to each other than do Germans and most Americans. In their interactions they are totally engrossed and intent on their discussions. On the sidewalks of the *grands boulevards,* one must watch out for the gesticulating French, who are so preoccupied with what they are talking about that they may not see you coming. When friends meet, they shake hands or embrace, gesture, and maintain the intense eye contact that enables them to read the other person's responses. In business dealings, however, they are more formal and restrained.

Of course, there are many regional differences in a country as large as France, with 55.6 million (1987 figure) people. In general those people living in Paris and in the north of France are more like other northern Europeans—more formal, with greater personal distance—than are residents of southern France, who have more Mediterranean influences and who stand and sit very close together in conversations and crowd together in cafes. Wherever one is in France, however, one is struck by the total involvement of personal interactions; people look at each other intently, they gesture and move together in sync, and they are totally engaged with each other to the exclusion of all else.

France As a Center of Art and Learning

Historically, France has been known throughout the world as a center of art and learning. French universities, especially the Sorbonne, have attracted scholars from many countries. Artists have always found France particularly stimulating, and France remains in some ways the cultural capital of the world, a center for architecture, painting, sculpture, literature, drama, fashion, and music.

Most general university programs are not oriented toward modern life or contemporary problems. Little in the curricula prepares students for a career in the business world. Instead, universities are directed primarily toward intellectual, political, and scientific pursuits, with particular strengths in engineering, atomic energy, medicine, and philosophy. Aesthetics and philosophy are revered by the French, who appreciate interminable philosophical discussions, brilliant rhetoric, intelligence, quickness, and sharp wit.

Business is not highly regarded in France. The high-prestige occupations are government service, medicine, law, and engineering, in that order. Graduates of the elite schools (*les grandes écoles*), top civil servants (members of the *Grands Corps de l'État*), university professors, artists, and writers generally enjoy greater prestige than do business executives. Highest respect is reserved for intellectuals because ideas are very important to the French.

Pride, Chauvinism, *Élan* and *Panache*

The French pride themselves on the art of speaking their language with great precision, fluency, and, on occasion, with true wit and brilliance. Indeed, the French sociologist Pierre Bourdieu once described France as "the country where husbands have been known to kill their wives over a point of grammatical usage." Repartee is greatly admired. Over and over again we have been told that the most important skill for any foreigner who wishes to function effectively in France is to learn to speak the language well.

93

The French revere ideas and literature, and they appreciate scholarly allusions and references. In fact, like the Germans, they tend to assume that if something is clearly written, it must be simplistic. They admire exotic, arcane, recherché writing, and scholarly tomes that only a knowledgeable few can understand.

The French have been very slow to learn foreign languages. For the French, the center is the position of power and importance, and France *is* the center. Why then should they have to learn a foreign language? At one time French was the language of most of the courts in Europe and the language of diplomacy all over the world. During its period as a colonial power, France required colonial administrators to learn French and insisted that instruction in all colonial schools be conducted in French. Within France itself, people speaking French with an accent are at a disadvantage even today. The French prefer that foreigners speak the language, but, unfortunately, most foreigners cannot speak French well enough to satisfy the French, especially the Parisians. Nevertheless, foreigners who make the effort to learn to speak French will have a distinct advantage.

Throughout their history the French have been wary of foreigners and foreign travel—a characteristic that has led outsiders to consider them xenophobic. When the French say "*tout le monde*" (literally, "all the world"), they mean either everyone who is French or everyone in their own social group. In recent years this has begun to change slowly as more French people read about other countries, learn other languages, and travel. The *Club Méditerranée,* a popular holiday club, has been a positive force in introducing the French to other parts of the world. It provides French ambience and French food and wine in foreign settings—permitting the French to explore the world from a safe base.

The French are a very proud people. They pride themselves on their many accomplishments throughout history and on their contributions to world culture. Their most successful leaders have understood the importance of pride and self-respect to the average citizen and have known how to flatter, cajole, and motivate people to cooperate and obey, a difficult task in a nation of individualists. De Gaulle in particular understood this well. After World War II he restored feelings of national pride and gave the French a sense of their own destiny; most important, he restored their sense of honor.

Directly related to their distrust of foreigners is French chauvinism. The French feel that France is the arbiter of all things important in diplomacy and prefer to go their own way in international relations. They are considered nationalistic by their neighbors and allies and are very clear as to their own primary objective: France first in everything. This attitude makes it very difficult for French government officials to work cooperatively with other nations, who are apt to regard the French as inflexible and uncooperative. France did not join NATO and more recently angered the United States government by refusing permission for its planes to fly through French air space en route to bombing Libya.

Style and élan are very important to the French. They try to do everything with verve and panache (flair). In general it's the overall effect that matters to the French, not the details. (What a contrast to Germany, where perfection in details is all-important!) When you walk into a French theater, you may be overwhelmed by its elegance and ornate decor: gorgeous chandeliers, plush carpeting, elegant antiques. But if you look carefully, you'll notice that the baseboards need painting and the seats are frequently rickety. The same cavalier attitude is also apparent in some French hotels. Even first-class French hotels may have quite different standards for maintenance from comparable American or German hotels. French hotel rooms may have thin doors with loose handles and decrepit furniture, but the rooms have such great charm that despite these deficiencies, the general impression is one of antique elegance. The French appreciate the overall effect and dismiss a bit of genteel decadence. This relates directly to the French preference in advertising; as we shall see, image in advertising is far more important to the French than factual details.

The French emphasis on style is also evident in the media, especially the newspapers. Literary style is highly regarded and is even more important for a French journalist than skill as an investigative reporter. Some top French journalists have been elected to membership in the *Academie Française,* an accolade bestowed on writers of outstanding literary ability. Americans, like Germans, prefer "in-depth reporting," digging out the truth behind the surface event. Not the French. They admire journalists who can write well and whose prose is replete with historical allusions and philosophical digressions. Discussing the reporting of an important political speech, an international journalist observed, "The French are as interested in discussing what the politician might have said or could have said as in what he actually said."

In a highly centralized society, it is easy for the government to dominate and influence the press. In France this influence extends to media distribution, advertising income (one government agency controls a major part of the advertising budget), and credit extended by government-controlled banks. The French press is also vulnerable to censorship because government officials can deny reporters access to government briefings if they step out of line.

Class Structure: The Hidden Hierarchy

The French move in very restricted social circles. Relationships begin with the immediate family, a tight-knit group that includes grandparents, aunts, uncles, and cousins, and may expand to include a few school or university classmates and long-time family friends. Major holidays and vacations are often spent with members of the family. This tiny circle is of great importance and offers stability, support, acceptance, and *tendresse* over the years. Social interaction with neighbors is usually limited and rarely leads to close friendships.

The French dichotomize their business or professional life and their private life, keeping the two totally separate. Socializing with professional colleagues is within the context of business and does not include one's family or one's private life. Because one's family life is very private, it is not considered polite to ask personal questions about an individual or her or his family. An invitation to visit the home of a business acquaintance is rare.

French society is highly stratified and is divided into clearly defined classes: *haute bourgeoisie* (or *grande bourgcoisie*), including a small elite of old, aristocratic families who still have power and influence, and the top professionals in business and government; *petite bourgeoisie,* high-level managers and bosses of small companies; *classes moyennes,* middle-level people such as teachers, middle managers, shopkeepers, and artisans; and, at the bottom, *classes populaires,* workers and low-level employees. The immigrés from former French colonies are a separate group. (If you want to understand the French hierarchy, we recommend Elias's *The Court Society;* see reading list.)

Membership in the aristocracy depends solely on lineage, not money. During the nineteenth century these aristocratic families disparaged commerce and tended to remain aloof from business, staying in their family *châteaux* or in their Paris apartments. As a result the haute bourgeoisie assumed leadership by default in both industry and government. Today French aristocrats live very quietly in a refined manner, shunning publicity or contact with those who do not belong to their circle. Although some are now impoverished, they are still highly respected.

The old families and other members of the haute bourgeoisie occasionally intermingle; haute bourgeoisie families who have achieved great financial success can often find aristocratic husbands for their daughters, provided the daughter has a sufficiently attractive income.

The aristocrats and haute bourgeoisie dominate the educational system, especially at the secondary and higher levels that are the gateways to career success. These families stress the importance of education to their children and begin early to prepare them for the examinations that will lead to entrance to the grandes écoles or the universities. This practice has led to the continuation of elites in French society. Access to the elite schools at both the secondary level (*lycées*) and the university level is restricted by a selection process which rules out virtually everyone who does not come with proper connections. Only a handful of outsiders or "not-authorized" individuals ever achieves entrance. At the moment, the French government is struggling to improve the availability of quality education, but no one can predict whether this reform movement will succeed. (See in the reading list Professor Ezra Suleiman's *Elites in French Society: The Politics of Survival* for an interesting discussion of this system.)

Working-class families live in a separate social world. Working-class adults are handicapped by their lack of education, and their children are prevented from entering elite schools because of inadequate background and education. Despite these differences in social mobility, the French worker is very proud, fiercely independent, and feels that she or he is the equal of every other French citizen, and, because of the French tradition of civic equality, need defer to no one. But the working-class French also know it is doubtful that their children will be able to attend schools that will prepare them for good jobs. This means the children may expect little social advancement since status depends on education and occupation.

Language facility is considered the mark of an intelligent, educated person, and those who are not in command of the highly refined language of the well-educated French and who cannot express themselves eloquently are seriously handicapped. Some working-class French people feel self-conscious about their speech. They are inarticulate in presenting their views in public or before government officials, particularly when confronted with someone of superior educational background. Then, there is also the matter of dialect and accent. Some accents, like those of the well-educated French, are highly regarded, while others are looked upon as provincial. The importance of the accent is similar to the situation in England, where one's accent is directly related to one's position (what linguists term "Oxford-received" English versus cockney, for example).

There is considerable hostility between social groups in France, and French labor is sometimes motivated by this underlying hostility in its dealings with management. The whole problem of labor relations in France is too complex for the scope of this book, but it deserves special attention from business executives hoping to succeed in France. A short summary of recent developments in the labor movement can be found in John Ardagh's *France in the 1980s* (see reading list).

Education: Gateway to Success

The operating principle of French education is negative reinforcement.

—French schoolteacher

The reforms that followed the student uprisings in 1968 have resulted in many changes in the French educational system, some of which are still occurring. Nevertheless, critics contend that the system's entrenched centralization leads to extreme rigidity. French education is still unresponsive to student needs. Some contend the French lack of responsibility for civic affairs stems from the absence of any experience in self-government in French schools. These critics argue that training in rhetoric and deductive reasoning tends to make French students conformist, theoretical, and uncreative despite their verbal facility.

The goals of French education are the transmission of knowledge and training of the intellect. French academic standards are high; discipline is strict; and teaching is deductive, rhetorical, and very concerned with style. Students are required to analyze and synthesize their material and are trained to be articulate.

Education is compulsory for children from ages six to sixteen. At the end of primary school, after conferences with parents and a review of the student's record, students and parents decide which school the student will attend for further training. There are technical schools for those who are not gifted academically, and there are the lycées, which prepare for university entrance examinations.

The technical schools prepare students for high-level blue-collar jobs. The academically oriented lycées prepare students for the baccalaureate examinations. *Le bac* is a rigorous series of examinations required for admission to the universities, and pressure and competition are fierce. *Le bac* lays great stress on general cultural background for both liberal arts and science majors and has eight options, five academic and three technical. The most popular and prestigious is the option for math, science, and economics, considered the best preparation for entrance into the grandes écoles.

Most French universities are overcrowded and lack adequate libraries, laboratories, and classrooms. It is not uncommon to see students sitting in the aisles or standing in the rear of lecture halls. Students complain about lack of contact with professors and often feel isolated and disappointed in their university experience. After the years of pressure in lycées to gain admission to the universities through a process of rigorous rote learning, many university students have difficulty working independently, and there is little help from professors.

Students also complain that the curriculum is unrelated to life outside academe. And, in fact, upon completion of their degree, students often find there are no jobs available, especially for those in liberal arts.

Tuition at the universities is minimal, but expenses for living accommodations, food, and books are so high that many students must live at home and commute to school. For many students there is little in the way of social life. Since there are very few state grants for support, students from working-class families have a particularly difficult time, which helps explain why only about 10 percent of university students are from working-class families.

In contrast to the average university, the five most prestigious universities—the *École Polytechnique* (X), *École Nationale d'Administration* (ENA), *École Normale Supérieure*, and the business schools, *École des Hautes Etudes Commerciales* (HEC) and *École Supérieure des Sciences Économiques et Commerciales*—offer excellent faculties and facilities, and they recruit their students from the top lycées, most often those in Paris.

At these special lycées, carefully selected students often have to work seventy to eighty hours a week. They forego all else in pursuit of admission to these top universities knowing that graduates of these elite schools are assured a career at the very top of their professions.

Only one student in twenty is accepted by the grandes écoles. These schools produce a very high proportion of the country's top administrators and engineers. Their graduates are a self-perpetuating class with a near monopoly on positions of power and influence in both business and government. They are the French equivalent of Britain's "old boy network." Many of France's political leaders are graduates of the top schools: de Gaulle, Pompidou, and Giscard d'Estaing, for example. In the words of one knowledgeable Frenchman, "The top schools are in reality a nursery for those who are 'authorized.' This 'authorized' group, through chance or design, has co-opted the school system."

Critics of these elite schools claim that their curricula are heavily weighted toward professional and technical training with very little emphasis on general culture, literature, or the arts and that they offer no exposure to the serious and complex problems facing French society.

The reason we have described the education system in such detail is to emphasize its vital importance in determining one's options as an adult in France. The kind of education one receives determines one's future even more than it does in Germany and much more than it does in the United States. There is no equality of opportunity in French education since it is impossible for all but the most brilliant, best prepared, and well-connected students to gain acceptance to the best schools and universities. Students from working-class or *bonne bourgeoisie* families are usually resigned to finding jobs at the lower end of the economic scale.

French Communication Style: Indirection and Eloquence

Compared to Germans, the French are eloquent and relish conversation. Conversations in the two countries are as different as night and day. Germans use a direct approach, and as a consequence, they are sometimes perceived by the French as being brutally frank. Germans also have a predilection for facts and details while the French indulge in small talk and like a little mystery in their dialogue. Since the French are high-context, they tend to leave some things to the imagination rather than spell out specific details. In general conversation, the French admire sophistication, erudition and nuance.

Because they are high-context communicators, the French prefer subtlety and tact to frankness and fact. They will often talk around the point they wish to make and sometimes the listener must be intuitive to discover the hidden message that is being communicated (in this the French remind us of the Japanese). However, the French (unlike the Japanese) do relish conflict and spirited discussions; but the rhetoric must be logical and well presented.

The French are not in the habit of getting right down to business. They must get a feeling for the general mood first. Whether it's an important conference or just a routine office appointment, the French want a proper interval of general conversation, a period devoted to getting to know the other person or catching up on what she or he has been doing. During a business luncheon, business may, on occasion, be discussed during the fruit and cheese course, but *never* at the beginning of the meal. Always allow the French to take the initiative; they will glide into the business at hand deftly, with charm and elegance. They find it jarring when people, Americans and Germans, for example, insist on getting right to the point. It breaks their rhythm to short-circuit the introductory phase. Their action chain is broken, and it is not possible to resume an action chain in the middle.

French Books, Articles, and Presentations

French presentations are often elaborate, loquacious, and emotional, filled with literary and historical allusions. The French love to enhance their main theme with embroidered digressions. Sometimes they choose to appear obscure and unclear in order to avoid being considered naive.

The French love of books manifests itself in the unprecedented popularity of the television show "Apostrophes," hosted by Bernard Pivot, the dean of French book critics. An appearance on Pivot's show is vital for any author aspiring to a position of influence as a writer. Because everyone who is interested in books watches his show, the impact of Pivot's weekly program is profound; the show attracts 15 percent of the Friday evening audience and exerts an enormous influence on publishers and book sales.

The French are avid readers, and authors enjoy prestige and status in France. The French book market is healthy and extensive: over twenty thousand bookstores, stationers, and newsstands sell books. Forty-four percent of adults read ten or more books a year, and 18 percent read at least twenty-five. The most popular books are on politics and history or are biographies; also favored are books on the social system and high-level exposés of misconduct in government and business. Best-sellers are usually well organized and replete with information.

In business presentations, the French like to provide masses of figures organized in complex patterns along with detailed background information. This is a result of their education, which stresses abstract thinking and the use of statistics and figures. Some foreign business executives have commented on the French habit of inundating them with financial data and all kinds of statistics, which to the Americans is more overwhelming than enlightening. The French are not fact-oriented in the same way that the Germans are; rather, they look for the *pattern* as expressed by the figures. Like all high-context people, they are seldom satisfied with the prepared summaries preferred by Americans. They want to make their own contexted synthesis.

All this is quite different from the direct, succinct American communication style, with its predilection for concrete examples along with the facts. It is also very different from the Germans, who need their facts accompanied by well-organized, in-depth background data. Germans often find French reports singularly uninformative and lacking in specific substance.

In summary, Americans, Germans, and French all need information, facts, and figures. However, each defines and uses data in different ways. Americans are primarily interested in "the bottom line." Germans want lots of examples with figures. The French are preoccupied with patterns and insist on synthesizing all the data themselves.

American presentations to the French should be informative, logical, and well organized. Content *is* important to the French. At least part, if not all, of the presentation materials should be translated into French, as a courtesy.

Logic: The Key to Reaching the French

Pragmatism, logic, and realism constitute a strong current in French culture. The French admire and respect logic because it is the basis of their thinking, implanted by their education and training. They understand what will work and what won't, and they like strategies that produce results.

In conversations with friends the French can become quite heated and even dogmatic or combative. They challenge and confront and relish playing the devil's advocate. This stance eventually leads to a revelation of their true feelings and can bring a sharing of innermost convictions if the friendship is long lasting.

104

The most persuasive argument to the French is always the logical, practical argument. Take one example from advertising:

One French executive who had worked successfully in both France and Germany had great difficulty persuading his French home office to use German-style ads in Germany for its French products. For many years he tried unsuccessfully to explain to his superiors why French ads had no appeal to Germans. "Germans don't care about mood or emotional appeal," he would say, but the French office could not believe this and continued running their mood-laden ads. Finally, he turned to logic: "Since German shopping hours are severely limited, Germans naturally prefer ads that are full of information and facts about the product. They are also very value-conscious. But because there is not enough time to shop around and compare products in the stores, Germans are in the habit of doing their comparisons on the basis of information gleaned from ads. It is logical, therefore, that if a French firm is to sell in Germany, it must provide the buyer with enough information so he can make up his mind." This approach reached his French superiors.

FRENCH PSYCHOLOGY

How can you govern a country that makes 365 kinds of cheese?

—Charles de Gaulle

The French are Latin in their behavior—much more influenced by early Roman and Mediterranean cultures than by northern European culture in their actions, emotions, and values. Historically, they were also deeply influenced by the Catholic faith, which teaches forgiveness. Among the French there is great variation in character, temperament, and personality. Nonetheless, there are certain common behavioral characteristics which we have observed over the years and which have been described to us in interviews. These characteristics include a strong preference for individuality over conformity; a tendency toward autocratic behavior; perfectionism in style and manners;

preoccupation with status, rank, and formality; impatience; inner conflicts between emotions and pragmatism or logic; pessimism; a sense of humor; traditionalism; and creativity.

The French are strongly individualistic. This means they are not always responsive to other people's needs. Nor do they respond to public pressure for conformity or to pressures from others as Germans do. Because they do not respond to group pressure, they are poor "team players." French education is centered around the individual. Their leaders—from Louis XIV *("L'état, c'est moi")* to Charles de Gaulle—embody this principle.

In France, individuality is highly respected and conformity is disparaged. This is an area in which the Germans and the French differ greatly. The French are impatient with conformity because they don't like to follow the crowd. We were told by one Frenchman that his neighbor had bought a white Citroen, and though he himself had wanted a white Citroen, he bought a black Citroen instead because he didn't want to be like his neighbor.

Procedures are taken less seriously in France than in Germany or the United States. If a rule or regulation gets in the way of achieving a goal, the French will try to find some way to circumvent it. This is in direct contrast to Germans, who are meticulous in following procedures. Procedures bore the French; they think they inhibit their creativity and impinge on their individuality. They tend to be disrespectful of the law. We once observed a Frenchman walking against the light in Paris traffic, wading out into midstream and jabbing his umbrella at the cars. When his companion reprimanded him for not waiting for the traffic light he replied, "No machine knows better than I when it's safe to cross."

As managers the French have the reputation of being autocratic, demanding, hard on subordinates, and thoughtless of their needs. In the words of a French executive, "We are much more authoritarian than Germans." This authoritarianism starts in childhood. In schools teachers are strict and exacting and insist on correct behavior as well as correct answers. At home,

French parents expect self-discipline, obedience, and good manners in their children. In adult life the French expect obedience from subordinates, creating a conflict in a people who place a premium on individuality.

The French drive for perfection is as strong as the German, but they differ in the areas in which perfection is expected. For the French, perfection is found in style; for the Germans, in the details. To Germans proper maintenance of one's possessions, order, keeping one's commitments, and staying on schedule are important. To the French following the proper form, doing things correctly, is at the top of the list. For example, a French meal is a work of art, a composition not unlike a painting. Everything must fit together to create a perfect arrangement: the different courses of the meal, the cuisine, the wines, the service, the flowers, the setting, and last but not least, the company. Once arranged, nothing must be allowed to disturb the symmetry of the occasion.

The French are very polite and meticulous about social forms, always using the proper approach in social interactions. They are very conscious of protocol, status, and titles, and they treat important people with deference, great politeness, and consideration. They expect precision in language and appropriate dress and behavior. Unlike Americans, they are not informal or casual. They are very courteous to visitors and expect the same treatment in return.

Related to the above is the French meticulousness in dress. Very conscious of appearance, they prefer expensive, well-tailored clothes. They look at everyone and comment on others' clothing and demeanor. They spend money on things that show: clothes, makeup, the *salon* in their home, their office furniture and equipment. Fashion-conscious French women buy chic clothes that are well made of fine materials, complemented by carefully coordinated accessories, all of which they display with panache. French posture and stance convey a certain formality and correctness.

Every engagement, be it social or business, begins with general conversation. Unlike the Germans, the French are adept at small talk. They stay informed about all current events and delight in discussing them; they particularly relish the latest gossip.

While frankness is a virtue in Germany, it can be a gaffe in France. Frankness or even directness in communication is to be avoided because the French prefer tact and indirection, which are considered the marks of politeness and good manners.

In describing the French, both American and French executives use words such as *proud, sensitive, and touchy.* A keen sensitivity to the protocol of introductions is another French characteristic, according to a highly placed French diplomat. It's very important that the person who makes introductions be of equivalent status to the people being introduced. Correct form in such matters is vital. Position at the conference table is also important; the person in the middle is in control. In business meetings, rank and position are very important, as are business titles. In business a person's title may mean more than salary and fringe benefits, something some Americans may find difficult to understand.

We were told by a German managing director that honor is more important than money to the French: "Given the choice of saving his honor by keeping his word, or of making a profit, a Frenchman is more likely to choose honor." Situations where it is your money and a French person's honor at stake should be handled with great caution and diplomacy.

Patience is not a virtue in France, which at least in part has to do with French tempo. The French move quickly, think fast, and act fast. To get a feeling for their fast tempo, watch them rushing around Paris, sometimes almost at a run.

The fact that the French are high-context also contributes to their impatience and their tempo. Like every other national group, the French expect foreigners to be just like them. Because the French make it their business to be highly contexted, they expect other people to be similarly well informed. Therefore, they don't give other people much information because to do so would be an insult. When seeking a decision, the French expect a simple yes or no answer, not a lengthy discussion of the background of the issue at hand.

Inner conflicts between emotion, pragmatism, and logic create many seeming contradictions in French behavior. The French are demonstrative; they show love and affection as well as displeasure and anger. French intensity is evident in discussions where they become tenacious in defending their own point of view. Theirs is a mentality that is attracted to highly detailed subjects and problems of great complexity. They can become fascinated or obsessed with a particular problem and will not give up until it is solved.

Paradoxically, the French, who can be coldly intellectual and cerebral in their approach to literature, art, and science, are just the opposite when something touches them deeply. At such times, they show emotion in their speech and most often in their nonverbal communication. In fact much of their communication is nonverbal. A great French favorite is Marcel Marceau, the brilliant mime. When he performs, audiences sit spellbound in total silence, and not a cough or a sigh can be heard. Marceau makes a tiny gesture that brings the audience to its feet, roaring with laughter. Moments later, when he depicts sadness, the audience becomes quiet and subdued. We've observed Marceau for twenty years, in several countries, but the response he elicits in France is the most moving we've ever experienced.

Several people have commented to us on the typically French attitudes of pessimism and cynicism. They tend to expect the worst of themselves and of other people, which makes them suspicious of everyone. As one French woman said, "I expect the worst of people and events. That way I'm not disappointed."

Despite this pessimism, the French rejoice in humor; you find it in everyday exchanges as well as in their literature, cartoons, and drama, and it is one of the most endearing qualities of the French. Wit and satire continue to delight them.

The French are great traditionalists, conservative in their approach and resistant to change. But although they are rooted in history and make frequent references to past glories *(La Belle*

Époque), in the last thirty years French society has undergone many changes. The shift from an agricultural to an industrialized society has brought changes to every facet of life. Today, the French are becoming more open to new experiences and to foreigners. Nowhere is this more apparent than in the *Minitel* revolution.

The world's first electronic telephone directory, Minitel, is provided free to French telephone subscribers; it offers instant access to all French telephone numbers and to 4500 consumer services, including rail and air schedules and reservations, information on social security and tax regulations, and even examination results for university admissions. Minitel's electronic directory service is provided by Telcom, a government agency that also provides free computers to the subscribers, who are charged $4 to $10 per hour for using the system. The success of Minitel has been astounding.

As recently as 1977 only one-third of French homes had a telephone. At that time, French telephone service was unreliable and telephones were thought intrusive and annoying. Alarmed by the lag in telephone technology and service, President Giscard d'Estaing made an improved telephone system a top national priority. Minitel was the result. By 1987 France had twenty-four million telephone subscribers, up from only ten million a decade before.

Far and away the most popular feature of Minitel is the *messageries,* the four hundred direct dialogue services through which subscribers communicate with one another. Many Minitel subscribers use pseudonyms to engage in ongoing dialogues with people on every conceivable topic, including romance. In her fascinating article, "The Sexy Computer" (see reading list), Justine De Lacy says that "the *messageries* are a response to a society that teaches people to be not only wary of strangers but also suspicious of friends, one in which a burden of rituals and rules regulates most activity." Minitel offers freedom to express ideas and emotions with no risk. One no longer need fear the hierarchy (social, economic, or academic); one can experiment and be free.

The impact of Minitel on French society is nothing short of revolutionary. Some French people are even giving up their lunch hour to stay in the office and use the Minitel computer. French sociologists are busy studying every aspect of this phenomenon, focusing on such cities as Strasbourg, where the population is delighted to be able to "reach out and touch someone."

Luigi Barzini feels that the French respect for individuality and their tendency to be quarrelsome have their positive aspects. He writes, "Perhaps France could not have become the great, admirable and endearing country it was and still is (in many ways *La lumière du monde*) had it been inhabited by uniform, dull, and docile people." For Barzini, the diversity within France has contributed to its creativity and balance.

FRENCH BUSINESS

Since 1986 France's GNP has slowly risen with more than 25 percent coming from exports, and a growth rate of 3.25 percent. However, at 10-11 percent, unemployment is a serious problem, even more serious than in West Germany or the United States. France and West Germany are the two largest trade partners in Europe; these two very different cultures are financially dependent on trade with each other and with the U.S. for their economic well-being.

Government and Business: Close Ties

Knowing the technical rules and regulations that affect business in France is the first priority for American business executives there. The offices of the French *Chambres de Commerce* in Paris and other French cities can be helpful. Also, the French government has a number of trade offices in American cities that provide voluminous documentation covering all aspects of doing business in France. Other good contacts for information on doing business in France can be found at the *Centres Accueils aux Industriels*.

France has a long history of government involvement in business. The *Banque de France* was established by Napoleon, and today there are still close ties between banking, business and government. For example, many of the most important banks were nationalized by Francois Mitterand early in his first term as president. In 1986, after a parliamentary election, Prime Minister Jacques Chirac announced a denationalization plan for fifty state-owned banks and major corporations, returning them to private ownership. This move sparked interest on the part of American and other foreign companies who want to establish businesses in France. This kind of shift in basic government policy following an election is one reason why personal ties between business and the highest levels of French ministries are vital.

There are many regulations that directly affect all business: currency regulations, price controls, national economic planning goals, and labor regulations. There are also influential, informal networks of personal contacts between government officials and business executives which are essential to conducting business. This network is similar to the one in Japan known as "the magic circle."

Personal Contacts: The Vital Early-Warning Networks

In addition to a thorough knowledge of French rules and regulations affecting business, American firms conducting business in France will need representatives in France who have *the right contacts*. In a polychronic country like France, personal contacts are crucial, and these contacts can be an early warning system of change.

People at the top levels of French government and business are often graduates of *les grandes écoles*, and they maintain school ties throughout their professional lives. This network enables its members to stay informed on important changes in the government or in the business community. Decisions are made at the top level of the French government that have far-reaching implications and a direct impact on business. Connections to the "old boy network" are usually only possible for those foreign companies that are very large, wealthy conglomerates (IBM, Ford, etc.). These companies, with their wealth and power, bring new employment, technology,and financing, which automatically insure access to influence networks. Small companies without such assets will find it necessary to hire people with connections. It is also advisable to establish good working connections with the *Préfecture* and *Conseils Generaux.* In the words of one experienced French businessman, "It is a deadly sin to ignore the *fonctionnaires* with whom you have to deal."

Bureaucracies: Designed to Defeat

> . . . foreign executives, American and otherwise, say that the French win hands down in the International Creative Bureaucracy Sweepstakes.
>
> —Philip Reuzin, *Wall Street Journal*

French bureaucracies are famous for their rigidity. Said one Frenchman, "Our bureaucracies are fossilized." There is a kind of stifling centralization in their bureaucracies and one can spend days, weeks, even months running from one French bureau to another.

French bureaucrats are reputed to be arrogant, sometimes rude, unobliging, and hidebound in their thinking. They infuriate the French as well as foreigners. The French, however, seem resigned to the frustrations involved while foreigners will persist in attempts to overcome them. In the words of one long-time observer of France, "French bureaucracies are designed to defeat."

Because of the national tendency to centralize everything, French bureaucrats take forever to get things done. Your French banker and your French lawyer should be consulted and can assist you in handling the bureaucracy.

One vice president of a German manufacturing company assured us that French bureaucracies *can* be mastered despite their complexity. His advice: "Study the French regulations. Break them down into components. Master the complexity. Reduce their regulations to procedures you can follow and you'll have fewer problems." Note that this is a very German approach.

Management Centralization: Command and Control

As we have mentioned before, French business is highly centralized. This often means there is one person at the top who makes critical decisions, which can be either an asset or a liability depending on the skills and experience of that person. In some companies you may find the director general achieved his position through marriage or connections, and he may be only a figurehead. In the case of a family-owned business, you may need to talk not only to the director of the company but to older relatives as well, even if they have formally retired. One French salesperson told us he not only had to sell the president of a company on his product, but the president's father and grandfather as well—both of whom had retired many years earlier but who still had power and influence.

In dealing with other businesses, French executives tend to go right to the top, in contrast to Germans who go to their counterpart within the other organization. In dealing with people at the middle level of French business, remember that if you come to an impasse, you can usually get around it by moving up in the hierarchy, a strategy taboo in Germany.

Women in French Business

Despite the fact that the majority of urban French women work outside the home, few women can be found in top management positions in French business, even fewer than in the U.S. Like American women, most French women are in low-level secretarial or clerical jobs. The few exceptions are mostly in the fields

114

of advertising, cosmetics, fashion, and art. French women do have some influence in intellectual circles and many are well-known writers and teachers.

Autocratic Behavior: "The Boss Is the Boss"

The French have a tendency to be autocratic in their business dealings. Several executives expressed the opinion that the French were even more autocratic in their management style than the Germans. French executives expect their subordinates to do exactly as they are told; employees must often work overtime at night and on weekends. Personal plans are secondary to the needs of one's immediate superior.

Because the French are both high-context and polychronic, they expect everyone to know how to do everything properly. They won't tell subordinates or colleagues anything, yet they get irritated if co-workers don't do something right. Such an attitude can be infuriating to foreign colleagues, particularly Americans. The French rarely compliment employees on their performance and are critical of any errors.

Because the French are high-context, general information flows freely. However, there is one important point to keep in mind. The French share specialized information *only within their own network;* often they do not share information with subordinates. We've had many reports of instances where the boss did not keep subordinates informed about important aspects of the business operations, with the result that major problems developed. In the stratified French society, subordinates are not in a French executive's network. Foreigners tend to perceive the retention of information as an example of French arrogance and interpret it as a power play. To deny information to one's subordinates is keenly resented by Americans.

We interviewed a European manager of a large French company who had worked in the United States for fifteen years for two different American firms. In one of his jobs he supervised eighty Americans in what he described as an overly bureaucratized situation in a company that favored consensus decision making. He said, "The American syndrome produces people who avoid decisions. Only at the end, when the obvious is perceivable by everyone, is consensus reached. This process takes too long and lacks creativity because there are too many participants. American managers make four major decisions: two are wrong, one is right, and one is in-between. The French manager makes hundreds of decisions. He fails ninety percent of the time but ten percent are good decisions."

Fear of Risk

Reluctance to take risks is another characteristic of the French, which can be very costly in the long run. Some French PDGs (*président/directeur général*) resist the notion of investing in capital equipment and improvements because they are in the habit of guarding every *sou*. If their business makes a profit, they are more apt to invest it in real estate or stocks, not in new machines or new plants. The Industrial Revolution came late to France and this fact, coupled with their natural conservatism, sometimes leads to a short-sighted view. An additional handicap is the French distrust of anyone they don't know personally, either French or foreigner; any proposal from outside the circle will be exhaustively examined by the French executive in charge.

Since the French tend to be cautious, taking time to reach decisions is for them a sign of patience and wisdom. Related to this caution are other highly valued business virtues such as continuity and security.

Commitments: Get It in Writing

A major problem for international businesses around the world is implicit assumptions about commitments. What is considered a binding commitment in one's own country may not be considered so in another.

Only written commitments are binding to the French. If you want to be sure of something, get it in writing. Never take a verbal or a telephone commitment as binding because the French may very well change their minds. An example of this occurred in 1982 when President Reagan thought he had an agreement with President Mitterand to establish allied economic policy towards the Soviet Union. At the very last minute, the French government announced it was dissociating itself from the allied policy.

One caution for American business: do not take at face value any financial statements or assurances about a French business without checking very carefully with your banker and your own financial experts. According to several executives, more than a few foreign business firms have suffered substantial losses because they believed French balance sheets when they bought French companies. A balance sheet can be written many ways, which is why the French themselves insist on seeing *all* the figures, not just a summary.

Formality: *Comme il faut*

As we mentioned earlier, the French insist on politeness and respect in business. They do not like informality, first-naming, or anything that smacks of familiarity or lack of respect. They expect people to dress properly and to observe all the social amenities. In particular the French object to hearty backslapping, joking or teasing behavior, or any kind of phony chumminess. Off-color stories in mixed company are absolutely unacceptable. Women are treated with politeness in both office and social situations. Etiquette is a traditional value that pervades French society, and business etiquette is symbolized by properly engraved business cards, giving a business title and academic credentials.

Beware the seeming informality of superiors at office parties. The French boss may appear relaxed on social occasions, but this facade of bonhomie has misled unsuspecting Americans to lapse from formal polite behavior into being overly familiar. The boss is sure to remember the next day. A French boss can be informal, but subordinates may not be, ever.

117

Meetings: Eloquence in Action

Everything about French meetings is different from American ones: tempo, style, and duration. Usually, the goal of the French meeting is to assess and brief the participants, to inform and be informed, to feel out people's reactions, and to encourage expression of opinions. Americans who go to French meetings with an agenda in hand, expecting it to be acted upon, will usually be disappointed.

French meetings have a fast tempo with prolonged discussions of many things. Participants are eloquent, and to Americans much of the eloquence seems to have little relevance. Ideas are presented and elaborated upon, sometimes in philosophical terms, which is why meetings may last two or three hours without any definite agreement being reached. If an agenda exists, it is seen as a beginning, not as an end in itself.

When the French attend meetings run by Americans they are apt to feel shut out or restrained by the agenda and the Americans' rigid adherence to schedules that allow little or no time for general discussion. The American meeting is linear, designed to cover specific points, reach decisions, and end punctually so that participants can make the next appointment on their schedules. There is little room for "open space" in American meetings, no time allotted for discussion of extraneous matters. This leads to frustration on the part of the French participants, who are likely to want time for items not on the agenda.

The Business Lunch: *Haute Cuisine* and *Savoir-Vivre*

Monochronic/polychronic differences pervade common interactions. The following encounter illustrates quite different attitudes toward what seems a simple thing—the business lunch:

German executive Herr Schmidt arrived in Paris for a nine o'clock appointment at a French company. When he reached the office,

118

the French manager he had come to see had not yet arrived. Schmidt waited and fumed; at nine-thirty the French manager and his subordinates appeared. After greetings and apologies, the manager ordered coffee and asked Herr Schmidt, "Where shall we have lunch today? Do you like fish or beef? What would you prefer?" The German deferred to his local colleagues, whereupon a spirited discussion ensued among the French: "How about the restaurant we went to last Wednesday?" "No, the cheese was old and the lettuce wilted." "Then perhaps the restaurant on the Left Bank where we went Monday?" "No, the sole was not as fresh as it should have been." After several more minutes of critique, while each French person made a contribution, a consensus was reached and a secretary instructed to make a reservation. Shortly thereafter, it was necessary to leave for the restaurant to avoid heavy noon-time traffic.

Lunch consisted of six courses with several wines. Conversation was lively and filled with current financial news and reports on various art openings, plays, and sporting events. Sometime after the fruit course, the French manager made a brief mention of business, but before Herr Schmidt could respond, the conversation went on to other matters and the lunch finally drew to a close.

Back at the office at three o'clock, a serious discussion began, punctuated by a relatively quick decision about where they would dine at nine that night. By five o'clock the German was exhausted and had missed his scheduled flight back to Frankfurt. He called his office and then asked his French colleague to reserve a hotel room for the night. He escaped to the hotel for a rest before being picked up at eight-thirty for dinner, and spent a long evening until midnight at another gourmet meal, followed by a promise of concrete discussions the next day.

The French business lunch provides an excellent example of how something that is not very important in one culture can be extraordinarily significant in another. In polychronic, high-context France, it is essential to maintain proper relationships with business partners. There is a deep need to get to know another person well enough to be able to predict how that person will behave in a variety of circumstances. There is also

119

a need to develop informal communications channels. One of the best ways for the French to get to know clients and business associates is to meet away from the office in pleasant surroundings, and lunch and dinner serve this purpose well. According to one study, the length of the average French business lunch is 124 minutes, while the average American lunch lasts 67 minutes! It's been our experience that some French business lunches, particularly those involving new relationships, can last up to three hours. Business dinners may last several hours after work, which may help explain why French executives are not always on time in their offices in the mornings.

For the French, the business meal has several functions. First, it is a message to the guests. The French take great care in choosing an appropriate restaurant and then selecting the menu and the wine to accompany it. They try to create the proper ambience for their meeting, and they want the meal to convey respect for their guests and pleasure in their company. For the French, dining is a ceremony to set the stage for doing business and is an important part of a vital action chain. How people relate is far more important to the French than having a scheduled agenda. Like a minuet, the process of rapprochement cannot be rushed. It must be reached in accordance with the French ideal of savoir-vivre.

French behavior concerning the time spent away from the office getting acquainted is hard to justify from the point of German culture which is a low-context, bottom-line, schedule-oriented culture. Such behavior is an affront to German compartmentalization and their sense of order. Germans also dislike the fact that the French do not separate business from pleasure, which Germans mistake as not taking business seriously.

Once you have decided to do business in France or with the French in the U.S., a strong commitment to do things the French way should accompany this decision. If there are chronic complaints from the Americans in France, the chances are that the Americans involved are not properly informed about how the French operate. It is essential to recruit employees who do not find French procedures, social customs, and savoir-vivre stressful.

A practical note: most of France is on vacation sometime between mid-July and the end of August. Many small shops close then. It is unwise, if not impossible, to schedule business meetings during this summer holiday period.

Negotiations: *Sang-froid* and Soft Sell

If you or your associates speak French well, do so in negotiations; even if your command is not letter-perfect, the French will usually appreciate your making the effort. If you are not confident about your language skills, then hire a highly-skilled interpreter, someone experienced in business negotiations, well educated, and very polite. Brief the interpreter thoroughly to make sure she or he understands the main points of your presentation.

These rules for negotiations with the French should help:

1. Be formal and polite at all times. Your approach should be low-key and scrupulously correct.

2. Before the initial meeting, prepare carefully. It's most important to be informed, well organized, and clear in your presentation. Stress facts and the rationale behind your position.

3. Present your points in a logical sequence, giving reasons for each.

4. Concentrate on the *explicit* content of your presentation. Bring French translations of any technical material, with copies for everyone involved.

5. Be clear about how your product or service will benefit the French; give tangible examples.

6. Be prepared for interruptions and digressions. The French love to debate and wax eloquent on all occasions.

7. Be prepared for prolonged negotiations and discussions. Don't try to rush things.

8. All agreements should be carefully scrutinized by your French attorneys. Only signed agreements are binding. Verbal assurances, particularly those from middle management, can be changed without notification.

Managers: Consummate Jugglers

The complexity of the manager's job in France is beyond what most Americans expect. The French manager has many varied responsibilities; first and foremost is to keep in touch with business and government networks. The manager must also supervise top personnel, keep abreast of changes in currency rates and government regulations, make decisions vital to the company's future, monitor sales, and oversee plant and manufacturing operations. The job is demanding. The hours are very long and include working nights and weekends. This is why French managers expect and receive high salaries. In an American company with a French subsidiary, the company manager must be someone who understands and accepts American business practices and procedures but also understands the culture and behavior of the French and how to motivate them.

For American companies with French operations it is important to establish a special contact at the American home office—one individual whose job it is to serve as a channel for all communication between France and the U.S. Most important, the person in this position should have direct access to the top level of the American firm. Avoid using parallel lines of authority, especially if one line is unofficial. This strategy will only confuse the French, who want to deal directly with the top level through one person they know well.

Deliveries

One of the practical difficulties that many of the Germans and Americans we interviewed have experienced, delayed deliveries from French suppliers, is related directly to a French cultural pattern. There are many reasons for delayed deliveries, labor strikes among them. However, quite often delivery is delayed just because the French are polychronic/high-context and can easily be swayed by requests for priority from someone with whom they have a close personal relationship. The following tale is typical:

> A French manufacturer agreed to provide a German chain store with men's summer sports shirts by June 1. June and July passed with no deliveries, despite many phone calls between Germany and France inquiring about the order. The shipment finally arrived in mid-September, much too late for the summer season. On top of this, the French sent black shirts even though the German buyers had told the supplier that black would not appeal to Germans. Not surprisingly, a long legal battle ensued.

The French way of circumventing this kind of problem would involve many visits from the buyer to the supplier, with appropriate meals and time to get to know each other. A personal relationship would insure preferential service. This contrasts significantly with the German pattern mentioned earlier where the delays in delivery tend to occur because there is a *lack* of communication as tasks are deliberately and discretely carried out.

Sales: Contact with the Customer

The importance of salespeople to French business can hardly be overstated. Everything hinges on the salesperson's success with people. As we have just emphasized with the delivery story, personal contacts count heavily since the French system calls for ongoing relations with customers that span many years. In some cases several generations of old-line companies have served the same customers. Salespeople know their clients' families, their outside interests and hobbies, as well as their business needs and preferences. Such long-term relationships cannot be developed overnight. Also, French salespeople "own" their customers. If a salesperson leaves the company or is fired, she or he can legally take the customers along (and usually does).

Employees: Individualists All

Most French executives and middle-level employees are well educated, with a strong general background and an appreciation of literature and art. Professionals are usually highly trained. On the negative side, some foreign employers find French employees difficult to deal with and lacking in initiative. They tend not to relate well to others; the French are too individualistic to be good team players. They don't always identify strongly with the company.

French executives are sometimes accused of refusing to delegate authority, and at all levels we heard comments about how the French withhold information from anyone not in their own network. Indeed, some French executives work in virtual isolation, yet they do keep in touch with their own networks.

In our interviews in multinational organizations, several American, Austrian, and German executives characterized the French as very difficult and sometimes unpredictable and unpleasant to deal with. One Austrian executive said, "On occasion the French can be brutal and rude."

In French business most clerical employees do not expect perfection in themselves or others, and few French employees have a strong drive to be correct in all details, which may be why many supervisors are so autocratic. The French need clearly identified targets and supervision, but they do appreciate and respond positively to compliments on their performance.

One knowledgeable French business executive in a multinational company told us that French executives work best in small groups. He succeeded in his business by setting up small multinational teams who worked together toward a common goal with great success. His advice was to be positive. For example, he would ask his teams, "What can we do to reach our target?" not, "Why aren't we doing better?"—which only generated excuses.

Managing French employees requires an inventory of skills and great patience. The most important thing to remember is that establishing good human relationships and giving positive reinforcement are necessary to motivate the French, as the following example illustrates.

Sketch of a French Businessman

This sketch of how a French businessman integrated two different approaches toward business—one high-context, one low-context—clearly illustrates not only the relationship of French character to business but how different French business firms can be.

The story M. Michel told us is true, although his name has been changed. Pay close attention to how he deals with the conflicts he faces and how he is motivated by the needs of people who are dependent upon him.

From 1961 to 1966 I managed one of the three departments of an old French paper mill in a very autonomous way, as though I were operating my own enterprise. The department, quite small and recently established, was my complete responsibility for five years. I started with 12 people; we grew to 115 three years after, with a profit. We were in the country, where employment was rare; young people used to leave for urban areas to find work. I felt responsible for helping the region and attracting youth. I felt responsible for them *to be happy*. I needed good administration and reasonable profits, but *just as a means*. I knew everyone and used to spend time in the workers' houses to share contact. I loved them and they loved me. We had an extraordinary *esprit de corps*.

When sales were slackening and inventories rising, I used to think, "This means my people are going to work thirty-two hours weekly instead of forty. This means Robert will not be able to finish the small house he is building before winter. This means Jacqueline, who lives twelve miles away, will not be able to come to work at

125

5:00 A.M. in her small car and will have to ride her bike in the frosty mornings. This means Marie-Thérèse, who is getting very pale right now, will not have the mountain vacation she needs. This means Maurice will not be able to afford his son's studies in Paris." Then I used to snatch up my sample case and dash to Paris to fight like a lion for the customers, to earn Robert's new house, to pour gasoline into Jacqueline's Renault, to give Marie-Thérèse better health, and to allow Maurice's son to get educated! When I came back with a full basket of orders, I felt with pleasure the *finalité* of my job. I never lived such happy years.

Later, I betrayed my "children," and I joined a large modern company as a marketing and sales manager. The French Division of Labor prevented me from any contact with the plant. I did not sell for Marie-Therese, but to perform my quotas. I learned a lot of things. I became much more efficient and much less happy.

At times I don't feel very well in my businessman's skin. When I appear in God's Court, I imagine this dialogue will take place:

"Daniel, what did you do on earth with the life I gave you?"

"Oh! Father God, I was extremely efficient!"

"You were what?"

"I mean I made profits. I respected my schedules and precosts and never missed my appointments. My quotas . . ."

"Well, Daniel, do you think I gave you a life to fulfill quotas?"

Note M. Michel's polychronic, high-context approach to his first job: his orientation, his involvement with and intimate knowledge of the people who were working for him, his feeling of responsibility to that part of France where his factory was located. Managers can't buy this sort of dedication, yet it is seldom understood or appreciated by those who are unfamiliar with the French. It is difficult for Americans, whose forte is cutting costs, to get an accurate perspective on the whole pattern of interpersonal relations and how it operates, all parts linked together, each reinforcing the other, each dependent on the other.

As the industrialization process proceeds, French business is drifting further and further away from the principles which M. Michel held sacred, away from concern for people and toward the American and German models of linear decision making as promulgated by the principles of "scientific" management. The French experience life as a whole: M. Michel epitomizes much of what is positive in French culture.

French Advertising: Eye-Catching Aesthetics

While the function of German advertising is to transmit information, the function of a French ad is to release responses—two entirely different functions.

French advertising is high-context. It is based on product name recognition. In many instances the buyer already knows the product. This is why you see simple, one-line ads like "Dubonnet" repeated over and over, or an ad for Remy Martin showing a half-filled brandy snifter. These ads are the essence of simplicity, yet they *release the right response* in the French.

French ads are designed to be visually attractive and eye-catching to get the attention of the buyer and are reinforced by repetition. This fits the French visual orientation to life and reflects their sensitivity to aesthetics, color, and design. The tone of the ad and the product are often congruent: perfume ads create an air of mystery and beauty appropriate for perfume. Automobile ads fit the French attitude toward automobiles. The French see automobiles as more than a means of transportation; they want a car which is *nerveuse* (responsive), which makes them feel peppy and lively or comfortable and affluent. They are not as interested in the mechanical details as Germans are.

The French are not always loyal to particular brands or stores. Because they are great comparison shoppers and because they have long shopping hours, they indulge in frequent price and quality comparison shopping for household products, food, and clothes. Therefore, French stores are filled with shoppers who do a lot of looking before they buy.

The French like American products because they are original, practical, and often represent the latest trends. There are many American products that are well known in France. Because quality is respected by the French, it is important that American goods be well made. Once a product has disappointed them, it is very difficult to persuade the French to try it again.

Problems in translating advertising copy from one language to another are well known. For example, General Motors' phrase, "Body by Fisher," appeared in a Flemish translation as "Corpse by Fisher." In China Pepsi-Cola's slogan, "Come Alive with Pepsi," appeared as "Pepsi Brings Your Ancestors Back from the Grave." But another, less well-known problem is ignorance of the proper advertising strategy in a foreign country. An ad that is effective in the U.S. will not necessarily be effective in France or, indeed, in any other country. Several American advertising agencies know the French market, understand French advertising, and know how the French communicate. Many agencies in France can also help you. Seek their advice; also show examples of an agency's advertising campaigns and the sales figures that followed the campaigns to a knowledgeable French person whose opinion you respect.

If you are in the American home office, pay attention to feedback from your local representatives in France. The most common complaint we have heard about American advertising is that the heads of French subsidiaries, be they French or American, have great difficulty persuading American headquarters to accept their advice about appropriate advertising in France.

Americans from the French Perspective

The following are representative quotations from our interviews, reflecting the attitudes of many experienced French executives who work with Americans. These observations reflect the basic differences between monochronic Americans and the polychronic French.

American vice presidents in Europe are not creative; they are too tied to their checklists. Success is not achieved by logic and procedure alone. Sixty percent of the time, maybe, but Americans forget about the other 40 percent that should allow for creative and innovative ideas.

American executives are reliable and hardworking, and often charming and innocent. But they are too narrow in their focus; they are not well-rounded. They have no time for cultural interests and lack appreciation for art, music, and philosophy.

Too many American executives are preoccupied with financial reporting. This syndrome produces people who avoid decisions. Only at the end when conclusions are obvious are decisions made by consensus. This decision takes too long.

Americans don't know how to present themselves. They sprawl and slouch and have no finesse.

The French from the American Perspective

In an article about foreigners working with the French, Pierre Beaudeux examined the reactions of Americans. Of the American respondents in this study, 85 percent said the French are methodical, 80 percent considered them competent, only 67 percent thought they behaved in a professional manner, and 58 percent thought the French didn't work as hard as Americans. Other American observations about the French included the following:

They don't delegate.

They are less mobile than Americans.

They are not team players.

They don't keep their subordinates informed.

They are very authoritarian.

They are not concerned about working conditions and salaries.

They are not interested in improving their skills or knowledge.

They don't feel a sense of responsibility for their colleagues.

They have a negative attitude about taking responsibility generally.

They are very sensitive to hierarchy and status.

They are primarily concerned with their own self-interest.

Advice to Americans Doing Business In France

American executives in France are like a boxer with a withered arm. They've never developed themselves.

—American manager of a French company

This section summarizes some of the key points made earlier, much of it based on the advice of American and French executives who have had demonstrable success in the French market.

Each type of business is a special case and each industry has its own character. There are also special reasons for sending particular people to work in a foreign country. In the United States, for example, sending people overseas may be a way of getting rid of them; this is a mistake. Except in very rare cases, it is more difficult to succeed in a foreign country than at home. Send the very best people available, consider their advice carefully, and then leave them alone.

In the U.S., it's possible to run a business based solely on power: money, influence, and reputation. It may not be the best long-range strategy, but it sometimes works for a while. However, in any foreign country you must redesign your strategy because you are working under different rules with different people; you cannot depend on your power base at home to help you succeed.

To do business in another country, you need technical competence, success in the domestic market, a variety of resources (human talent as well as economic resources), and a commitment to get along with your foreign partners. In France you will need one more very important skill: fluency in the French language. Americans working with the French must speak their language or their business will suffer.

Some guidelines to be considered when working with the French are the following:

1. *Choose your foreign representatives with care.*

One of the most difficult tasks is finding the proper representative, who might be either French or American. To be competitive, you may have to pay more than you are used to paying. Because you are dealing with a scarce commodity, an effective foreign representative, you may find it worthwhile to increase your budget for salaries and widen your field of choices. To find the best people, consult your American bankers and your bankers in France as well as your French lawyer. Then, double- and triple-check every recommendation you receive. Executive search firms that specialize in finding experienced executives may help, but these firms are uneven in their performance, so check them very carefully. First, see how well they fill demanding, but not strategic, positions.

Representatives with the proper connections to influential networks are essential to your business success. Your representative should be able to mobilize talent and find people with demonstrated skills in your particular business. In addition, the candidate should have impeccable personal and professional qualifications. Find individuals who operate from a position of power and influence within their own specialty. Take your time in the selection process and check with knowledgeable people in France.

The question of whether your representative in France should be American or French depends upon how much you are willing to pay, conditions of employment, the qualifications of the individual, and the talent available. Sometimes someone who is not French but is from another European country will have more to offer for the money. If your representative is American, it is absolutely essential that she or he speak French fluently, understand French society and customs, and have years of experience in France. If your representative is French, she or he must speak English and be familiar with American business practices, particularly procedures and schedules, since interfacing will be an important part of the job.

2. *Build long-term, personal relations with the French.*

To succeed in business in France you must build lasting relationships with people. Keep in mind that your French distributors and your French salespeople spent years building up personal contacts that are vital to their business, so don't expect instant results either from them or anyone else. On the job you must develop a personal relationship with someone who will tell you exactly what you must do. The French don't provide job descriptions.

3. *To sell a product line in France, first you must sell yourself.*

Your first job is to sell yourself as a person to your French counterparts. Next, you sell your service, then your product and, after that, you sell your price. Your sales staff is the most important factor in your organization—even more important to success than advertising. To sell in France, you must become very French. When your representative starts explaining things in terms of the French mentality, it is bound to sound alien and strange, but you must expect this—and listen.

4. *Allow more time for everything in France.*

Remember that meetings in France are for the purpose of getting to know people or encouraging discussion, not for reaching immediate decisions. Meetings take more time, and there will be more of them before you reach the point of decision making. Be sure your French employees are offered an opportunity to voice their concerns, participate in meetings, and make their points even if those points were not originally on your agenda. Otherwise, they will feel shut out and resentful.

132

Many other things take longer in France than in Germany, and, as we said previously, you can expect delays in deliveries. You can minimize this by hiring a manager who knows your needs and who also knows how to motivate the French to meet deadlines. This may require funding numerous visits to suppliers to see how things are going, performing on-the-scene stroking to ensure that your orders get top priority, and being able to find out in advance if delays are inevitable. It would be a mistake to discourage or to try to reduce such visits merely to save money.

5. *Handle French employees with care.*

Remember that the French are great individualists. They work in highly centralized organizations with many information networks. They do not compartmentalize as much as Americans do, although they don't always share information on the job. They are polychronic, high-context, and autocratic. Managing French employees requires tact and skill. Never criticize, keep a light touch, consider feelings and pride. The French are not natural team players, nor are they perfectionists in business, but they like variety in their work and a chance to show creativity and originality. Since French employees respond positively to compliments, the American manager should be ready to reward satisfactory performance and show appreciation for employees' efforts.

6. *Remember that French business behavior is extremely situational.*

It is sensitive to immediate circumstances and responds to them. For example, we have noticed that when we go to small markets in Paris for a few purchases, it is best to go during the slack periods, not just after opening or just before the lunch-hour closing. Since we do not speak French rapidly and don't have all the required situational dialect, it takes us longer to complete our transactions than it does French customers. When they are not rushed, the store clerks are polite, but if you go at peak periods, you may be treated rather rudely—this is situational behavior (and, incidentally, illustrates the importance of fluency in the language).

7. *Give your advertising a French flavor.*

Listen to the advice of your French representatives about advertising. The French respond to image in advertising and to glamour, beauty, and humor. In planning your French advertising campaign, consult advertising agencies with experience in France.

8. *Educate yourself about France.*

France is a large, diverse, and interesting country with a great past and many centers other than Paris. It pays to deal with each center separately. *There are significant regional differences* just as there are class differences, and it requires study and extensive travel to get to know the country. In addition to speaking the language, it is a good idea to read widely and keep informed; the French are very interested in current events.

9. *Educate yourself about the business climate.*

Know your competition, your market, your legal and financial status, the media, and the labor force. Virtually any personnel changes you may want to make can cause costly delays if not handled properly. The French government is constantly making changes in policies affecting your business. This is why your French representative must have lines to people in power to keep updated.

10. *Support good management practices and build personal relations.*

People are your most valuable asset. Since people produce, distribute, sell, and make up the working core of every organization, and are also your customers, there is nothing more important than learning how to reach people. This means motivating them, inspiring them, directing them, providing them with opportunities, and making friends with them. No organization can survive without the active participation and help of the people who staff it.

Above all, avoid the "do-it-our-way" approach; it won't work.

The Germans and the French

Despite the fact that Germany and France are close neighbors who have interacted for centuries and are today economically interdependent, there is little real understanding between the two countries.

The Germans, with their precise scheduling, slow pace, insistence on procedures, and deliberative decision-making process, drive the French crazy. French delays in deliveries, failure to submit routine reports on schedule, and their tendency to interrupt work schedules and break action chains infuriate the Germans. None of these misunderstandings contributes to a productive working relationship; indeed, it is highly stressful for people in both countries.

The highly territorial Germans barricade themselves behind closed doors to insure unbroken concentration. They seek order in everything and are careful to observe rules and regulations in public and in the office; they constantly correct each other. In contrast, the French are open to interruption to insure high-information flow and keep themselves informed by cultivating a large network of clients, friends, and acquaintances (who might transmit valuable information). They have an autocratic management style, centralized, top-down decision making, and one of the world's most infuriating bureaucracies.

The people in both these countries pay attention to details; the difference lies in their focus on those details. The Germans observe schedules scrupulously, attend meetings promptly, meet deadlines for reports, and fulfill obligations to the letter. The French pay close attention to personal appearances, the appearance of offices, and the entertainment provided clients. Most important, they pay very close attention to the vitally important information networks.

The Germans are irritated by the French emphasis on savoir-vivre, which interferes with serious business; the French think the Germans don't appreciate or enjoy the good things of life: haute cuisine, humor, wit, or good conversation. They are especially annoyed by the German habit of coming right to the point before proper social amenities have been observed.

People of every country and every culture have similar problems with foreigners, whom they feel are somehow deficient in the qualities they themselves value. It is our hope that by presenting some of the underlying structures of culture, people will begin to realize that everyone is caught in the web of one's own culture.

Culture determines what we perceive, how we react to situations, and how we relate to other people. Understanding the basis of some cultural differences may help people not to react personally to behavior they don't understand. Perhaps, instead, they can begin to see beneath the surface to find out why others act as they do. This discovery leads to appreciating the rich diversity that exists on earth and the genius and variety of all humanity. In the end, it is only by understanding others that we gain insight into ourselves and our own culture. The United States has many different cultural and ethnic groups; it abounds in people who are high-context, low-context, monochronic, or polychronic. Americans too have much to learn from each other. An understanding of different cultures may well be our own most important asset in meeting the challenges of our times, both abroad and at home.

PART 4

The Americans

The size of the United States as well as the ethnic and regional diversity of the population make it difficult to generalize about Americans. The variety is far greater than in Germany or France. When we use the term Americans, we refer to those people whose forebears came to the U.S. from northern Europe, the predominant group in American business today. Most of the people we interviewed for this book were well-educated individuals from middle- or upper-middle-class backgrounds, and many of them had lived and worked all over the U.S. We conducted interviews in New York, Washington, D.C., Chicago, Los Angeles and San Francisco. Prior to conducting the interviews, we had worked with American business for over thirty years in many parts of the U.S., including small communities. We want to remind our readers that there are many different regional and local business practices which are beyond the scope of this book.

AMERICAN CULTURE

> The U.S. is not a melting pot: ethnic groups persist. Nonetheless, Americans feel a bond to other Americans that transcends differences in ethnic origins.
>
> —Jackson Toby, "America Works Despite All the Odds"
> —*Wall Street Journal*

Like people all over the world, Americans take their culture for granted. Indeed, it's only in juxtaposition with other cultures that Americans begin to understand the influence of their own culture on their behavior. Only when we can see that there is more than one approach to life and many different ways of behaving can we begin to experience the strong, pervasive influence of our own culture.

It is more difficult to describe American culture than German or French culture because the United States is not just another country; it spans a continent, and has a population of over 250,000,000 people whose ancestors came from virtually every country in the world. American culture is a rich mix of Anglo-Saxon, French, German, Scandinavian, Spanish, Italian, Latin American, Native American, African, Polish, Russian, Japanese, Chinese, Korean, Filipino, Vietnamese, and Arab influences, just to name a few. In its early days the country was strongly influenced by the British and other people from northern Europe; its laws are based on British common law and American English has absorbed many northern European words.

Since this book focuses on business between the United States, Germany, and France, we have concentrated on the culture of the majority of American business executives, which can best be described as that of Americans whose forebears came from northern Europe. In a recent Gallup survey made for the *Wall Street Journal,* 65 percent of Fortune 500 executives as well as 68 percent of small-business executives were in this category. While the U.S. is a nation of immigrants and there are many people in American business who are not of northern European heritage, for the purposes of our discussion of Ameri-

139

can culture, it is the American-European culture we refer to and not the many other cultures represented in the American population. This dominant or mainstream business culture is the norm to which people with other cultural backgrounds are expected to conform, particularly in large corporations.

Despite its ethnic diversity, the U.S. has managed to absorb bits and pieces of many cultures and weave them into a unique culture that is strikingly consistent and distinct. You can pick out Americans any place in the world, often very quickly, because of their behavior. Among their most observable traits are openness, friendliness, informality, optimism, creativity, loudness, and vitality.

In common with others, Americans tend to be ethnocentric, in part because of the great size and economic power of the United States. Unlike the Germans and the French, Americans do not have close foreign neighbors with whom they interact constantly. The country shares borders with Canada and Mexico, but relatively few Americans have dealings with or know much about either country.

While the United States has absorbed millions of people from countries around the globe, the *core culture of the United States has its roots in northern European or Anglo-Saxon culture.* As a result, it is a predominantly monochronic, low-context culture. To succeed in the American economic system, people must adapt to schedules and the other conventions of doing business in a monochronic, low-context environment. It also means their approach to life is compartmentalized and they need detailed background information because they do not have well developed information networks.

Time: One Thing at a Time

The majority of Americans are monochronic, especially in business. This means that for them time is scheduled and compartmentalized so that people can concentrate on one thing at a time. Schedules are sacred and time commitments are taken very seriously. There are polychronic Americans, usually from families with origins in Latin America, the Mediterranean countries, or the Middle East. They handle time differently and are neither prompt nor necessarily scrupulous in observing deadlines. There are also regional variations in the handling of time. In the Northwest, South, and Southwest, for instance, the rules governing punctuality are more relaxed.

In their business and professional lives, however, most Americans adhere to the monochronic norms of Anglo-Saxon culture. Promptness is sacred, especially where business appointments are concerned. Being five minutes late calls for a brief apology; ten or fifteen minutes needs a more elaborate apology, or, if possible, a telephone call warning of the delay.

American time and consciousness are fixed in the present. Americans don't want to wait; they want results now. They move at a rapid pace; everything about their business lives is hurried. Wanting quick answers and quick solutions, they are not used to waiting long periods of time for decisions and become anxious when decisions are not made promptly. This attitude puts them at a disadvantage in dealing with people such as the Germans, the Japanese, and Latin Americans, all of whom, for different reasons, take more time to reach decisions.

American planning intervals are shorter than those in Germany and many other countries as well. Since most American companies are publicly owned and must report all financial details quarterly for use by banks, security analysts, and the government, American businesspeople tend to think in short-term intervals. When Americans talk about the "long term," they usually mean no more than two or three years.

Space: Keeping Your Distance

The size and scale of the United States and the feeling of open spaces are overpowering to visitors who are accustomed to the smaller scale of Europe. There is an expansiveness to the American character that is undoubtedly related to the geographical size of the country and to the lively frontier spirit that runs through American history.

Many Europeans comment on how large American apartments and homes are. The separate bedrooms Americans provide for each of their children and the other special rooms set aside for adult use often surprise Europeans and attest to the value Americans place on individuality and personal privacy. Americans are proud of the amount and kind of living space they have and will show visitors around the entire house, something unheard of in France and Germany.

Like Germans, Americans avoid close physical contact and keep their distance when conversing, automatically adjusting their chairs to a comfortable range. French conversational distance is closer than either the German or the American, which causes discomfort to the latter two. During conversation Americans maintain eye contact while listening but shift their eyes away and back when they speak; this level of eye contact is much less intense than that of the French. Americans gesture only moderately with their hands and arms, but their faces tend to be quite animated. Americans smile a lot in greetings and during formal introductions; except in large cities, they occasionally even smile at strangers they pass in the street. A strong handshake is the norm among American men and is associated with masculinity.

Although some American business executives have an "open door" policy to encourage the idea of accessibility, they do prefer private offices to working together in large open spaces, which they find distracting. Remember that monochronic, low-context Americans are vulnerable to interruptions.

Education in a Changing Society

One of the great differences between the U.S. and its European counterparts is the quality of public education. Critics of American schools have described them as training grounds for taking standardized tests and claim that education in the fundamentals of literacy is relegated to a secondary function. They also say that the average American public school curriculum overemphasizes memorization and that it encourages verbal expression but provides little training in written expression. It is generally agreed that the quality of public education has declined markedly over the last few decades. There are many reasons for this decline, which we discuss at some length because they reflect larger problems in American society and culture.

Americans want to provide the same basic education for all children from the first through the twelfth grades. This is a difficult goal because many students come from families where English is not the primary language or where the importance of education as a requirement for success is not understood. American schools also offer more extracurricular activities and more time is devoted to sports, clubs, music, and drama (and hence less to studies) than in European schools. Most important, in the authors' opinion, in American public schools there is no strong tradition of hard work and regularly assigned homework. Studies indicate that American children spend more hours per year watching television than they spend in school. The American school year is short compared to that of West Germany and France. Finally, the standard American curriculum is much less demanding than the German or the French, especially in mathematics, sciences, and languages (only 15 percent of American high school students study a foreign language). The results of American public school training are shown in studies and comparisons. Among twenty industrialized countries, American students ranked as low as eighteenth in some mathematical tests and no higher than tenth in any others. A study in the state of Illinois found 90 percent of high school graduates scientifically and technologically illiterate. Sixteen percent of all white adults, 44 percent of blacks, and 56 percent of native Hispanics are either functionally or marginally illiterate. Most shocking to us, the U.S. ranks forty-ninth among the one hundred fifty-eight members of the United Nations in literacy levels.

Unfortunately, there is a nationwide shortage of qualified, experienced teachers. Teachers are poorly paid compared to other professionals, and their social status is low compared to their counterparts in Europe. Low salaries and the overwhelming bureaucratic demands made on teachers have made teaching unattractive as a career for many Americans; the results are over-large classes and little individual attention to each pupil.

Another very serious problem in the American school system is the use of drugs. In junior high and high schools, drug use is common. There are some community and government programs designed to combat drug use, but it remains a major problem.

Dissatisfaction with public schools in the U.S. has driven many middle-class families to send their children to private or church-supported schools in the hope of providing them a better education. Most private and parochial schools have higher academic standards and insist on daily homework. Their student bodies are smaller and entrance standards usually more selective.

The authors recommend two recent books on the crisis in the U.S. educational system: *The Closing of the American Mind* by Allan Bloom and *Cultural Literacy* by E.D. Hirsch. Both offer useful insight into American culture.

Mobility: A Nation on the Move

Americans are highly mobile. Statistics indicate that the average American family moves every four to five years; many American business firms transfer employees every two years. This frequency of moving means that Americans are forced to meet and interact with strangers and learn to make new friends easily. It also helps explain why many Americans form superficial relationships more often than deeper and more lasting ones. Sometimes the surface friendliness of Americans creates expectations among non-Americans that close friendships will develop, but more often than not, these expectations are disappointed.

In the suburbs and in small towns, being a good neighbor means maintaining your property; lending tools, supplies and assistance; visiting across the fence; working together on projects; and sometimes trading invitations for coffee or dinner. Newcomers are generally welcomed with gifts of food, offers of assistance, and invitations to meet other neighbors.

In a society of ethnic diversity and high mobility, a "nation of strangers," many Americans suffer from an absence of roots. Perhaps this is one reason why many Americans find their identity in business or professions and in the civic organizations to which they belong—organizations such as the Rotary, Kiwanis, Elks, Lions, Jaycees, P.T.A., Junior League, Garden Club, and the Chamber of Commerce. These civic and business organizations perform a variety of community services but they also provide their members with a feeling of community, rituals of recognition, and rewards for outstanding performance. Americans like the feeling of belonging to a group that works together toward the achievement of common goals.

Work Ethic

Many Americans are still motivated by a strong work ethic which the early settlers from northern Europe brought with them when they came to the American continent. Europeans often observe that Americans schedule everything except time for relaxation. This is particularly true of American executives, who drive themselves hard, often at the expense of their families and their health. Americans have fewer holidays and take shorter vacations than do Europeans. Senior American executives often work fifty-six hours a week and take only fourteen days of vacation per year. In the opinion of many German and French executives, American executives are obsessed with work; "they're workaholics" was a comment we heard often. Like most Europeans who do not accept working on weekends or holidays, the Germans and the French reserve these times for themselves and their families.

Immigrants from East and Southeast Asia and elsewhere have also brought with them their own culture-based work ethic.

145

However, in the American population as a whole today, the work ethic as a motivation appears to be diminishing, especially among younger Americans, while a stronger orientation toward material or other social and personal rewards is becoming more evident.

Communication Style

Americans do prefer directness in communication, although they are not as frank or blunt as Germans are. Americans are often uncomfortable with indirectness and sometimes miss nonverbal cues: subtle shifts in voice; slight, almost imperceptible changes in body posture or breathing. This failure to perceive or understand nonverbal cues means that Americans often miss a build-up of tension in people such as the French, and, as a consequence, fail to realize that something is wrong until a crisis develops.

Bragging and boastfulness are common among Americans, and there's a lot of informal jockeying for position in American groups. They tend to exaggerate, much to the distress of the Germans, and they enjoy writers who tell "tall tales."

In manner, Americans are not as serious as Germans and often use humor to diffuse tensions on the job and in social situations. Jokes are relished and a good sense of humor is much admired. Most Americans keep their social conversations light, rather than engaging in serious, intellectual or philosophical discussions, a trait which especially bothers Europeans. Generally, Americans have little interest in discussing philosophy—either traditional philosophy or political philosophy. They consider philosophy too theoretical or abstract.

AMERICAN PSYCHOLOGY

I respect the American frontier spirit. Recently I met someone who drove 3,000 miles to find a job.

—Japanese automobile executive

146

The American dream is often a very private dream of being the star, the uniquely successful and admirable one, the one who stands out from the crowd of ordinary folk who don't know how.

—*Habits of the Heart*

The American and European cultures focus on the individual, in contrast to other cultures such as the Japanese, where the focus is on the group. Americans are outwardly oriented; concerned with appearances; preoccupied with what other people think, do, and say about them; and eager to be liked and accepted. Above all, they are individualists. Many are ambitious, hardworking, competitive, confident, and direct. They are usually egalitarian to the point of being quite casual in their manner and are pragmatic and sometimes simplistic in their approach to problems.

Americans pride themselves on being fiercely individualistic. They want to be "their own person." They are much more concerned about their own careers and their personal success than about the welfare of the organization or group. For Americans, it's "every man for himself."

Their strong bent toward individualism is directly tied to the value Americans place on freedom in all things, not just political freedom to vote as they wish, or religious freedom, or freedom of assembly, or freedom of the press but a vast array of individual rights protected by the American Constitution and the Bill of Rights. In addition, Americans expect freedom of choice in virtually everything. They are free to marry the person of their choice with little or no interference from their parents, free to choose whatever job or profession they wish, free to attend the college of their choice if they are accepted and can afford it. Individualism and freedom pervade every segment of American society and explain why for anything one can say or write about Americans, there are bound to be many exceptions. The great degree of freedom in the United States extends to all aspects of an individual's behavior. For young people there has never been a time of greater choice in terms of careers or lifestyles, which presents problems for some, who have so many choices it often takes them years to settle on a career.

Many Americans have little actual faith in political ideologies beyond the basic tenets of democracy. Nevertheless, they are patriotic, proud of their country, and believe strongly in democracy. Too much power and authority is considered unwise or even dangerous by Americans. Politicians who appear to seek power for its own sake are even more suspect than those seeking office for economic gain. As a result, politicians are especially adept at presenting an image of a "good old boy"—a submissive posture that diffuses the voter's hostility toward anyone with power and influence. For the same reason, Americans like to poke fun at symbols of power, and they tell jokes about their political leaders incessantly.

Government is viewed as a necessary evil and is generally disliked and disparaged. Most Americans think their government is too large and that control over people is immoral; they like to quote Lord Acton: "All power corrupts and absolute power corrupts absolutely." This distrust of authority leads to a certain ambivalence since Americans also admire decisive leaders. Given their attitude toward government, it is not surprising that many Americans take a dim view of politics and politicians. In fact, many Americans want nothing to do with political life, the result being a kind of apathy on the part of the American electorate. In a 1984 article, columnist Flora Lewis pointed out that in West Germany's last election, 89.1 percent of voters cast ballots; in France, 85.8 percent; in Britain, 72.7 percent; in Spain, 79.6 percent, in Italy, 89 percent. In the American presidential election of 1984, however, only 52.9 percent of eligible voters cast their ballots; and in 1988, only 50.16 percent voted.

Basically, Americans are practical people who like challenges and enjoy solving problems. They pride themselves on being pragmatic. They like to handle their own problems and they chafe at authority. In business and professional life Americans are ambitious, competitive, and hard-driving. Once they reach a goal, they set another. In negotiations they like to win, which explains the popularity of books such as *Looking Out for Number One* by Robert J. Ringer.

Most Americans admire hard work and success, and they don't feel ambivalent or hesitant about enjoying it. Their strong drive for recognition—as evidenced in their stance, dress, posture, attitude, voice level, and possessions—is one of the reasons why Americans are readily identifiable anywhere in the world. Their heroes are public figures who frequently appear in the press and on television: outstanding athletes, Hollywood actors, television stars, even business leaders.

One of the terms most often used by German and French business people to describe American business executives is "self-confident." Overseas Americans feel confident that their ways are the best ways and often demonstrate messianic zeal about imposing them on other cultures and then fail to understand why they encounter resistance and resentment. In addition to an overconfident attitude, Americans suffer from a tendency to dichotomize, to see things as "all black" or "all white" and therefore are either "for" or "against" something, often without fully examining the alternatives. In general, they tend to oversimplify and to look for instant solutions, which in part accounts for the American reputation for naivete in the rest of the world. They are often more interested in the headlines and the bottom line than in what comes between.

Many foreigners comment on the American low-context, legalistic approach to things; everything is spelled out and put on paper. Two-thirds of all the lawyers in the world are practicing in the United States; there is one lawyer for every 355 Americans, and litigation has become a way of life. Consumers are increasingly inclined to sue for damages when they feel they have been harmed by a product.

Within the American system of justice, there has been a preoccupation with protecting the rights of the individual, especially those accused of a crime. Critics of the system say the victim is too often forgotten, and American lawmakers and the courts are moving slowly to rectify this imbalance.

Americans value fairness, which means treating people impartially and without favoritism. They believe in equal opportunity for all and in equality before the law, that is, justice for every person regardless of social or economic circumstances. However, while most Americans profess a belief in tolerance and democratic ideals, women and minorities still face enormous barriers to achieving acceptance of their rights despite some progress in the past forty years.

Consistent with their egalitarianism, most Americans are friendly, outgoing and informal. They dislike being made to feel inferior and bristle at any system of arbitrary social ranking independent of achievement. They are uncomfortable with class systems such as those in France or England. The American belief in equality makes Americans dislike those who act superior or condescending or who attempt to "pull rank." Even influential people usually make an effort to appear approachable. For example, the manager who puts his feet on the desk, works in his shirt-sleeves, and invites everyone to call him by his first name is trying to show that he too is a member of the team. These efforts to create an egalitarian atmosphere are often offensive to foreigners, who decry the American lack of formality and manners.

American informality is partly a reflection of the egalitarian society and the absence of a formalized class system. The frequent use of the first name in addressing others is an example of this informality. The use of the last name, preceded by Mr., Ms., Mrs., or Miss, is a sign of respect reserved for older people, new acquaintances, or those to whom one wishes to show deference (a customer being served by a clerk, for example). Many Americans use the first name before they even know the other person, a habit most Europeans deplore.

This constant use of first names extends to business organizations at all levels—among peers and with subordinates—including secretaries, assistants, clerks, and service personnel. Titles are seldom used; the only people who are routinely addressed as "Doctor" are physicians, dentists and veterinarians. Most

Ph.D.s, unless they are very well-known, are only called "Doctor" in academic settings. This is not true in Europe.

In formal introductions Americans shake hands; they do not shake hands with co-workers at the office every day, as Germans do. In social situations, some Americans shake hands; others hug or kiss friends of the opposite sex by way of greeting; women often embrace; and men sometimes clap each other on the back. Most Americans do not, however, touch other people unless they are friends or relatives.

Even though Americans are very informal, they do value good manners and proper social behavior. They say "please" and "thank you" frequently or sometimes just "thanks" with a smile. It is considered polite for American acquaintances and friends to inquire about each other's families when they meet. Recently, there has been renewed interest in etiquette books and newspaper columns that offer advice on social courtesies after a decade of relaxed rules during the 1960s and a gradual move toward formality during the 1970s (see *Time* article, "Minding Our Manners Again," in reading list). Good manners are more highly esteemed in some social circles and geographic areas than in others. Cities such as Boston, Washington, Charleston and Atlanta—and in the South in general—tend to be more formal because, although there are no formal class distinctions, there are "old families" that emphasize polite behavior. However, some Americans prominent in business, politics, and the professions lack the manners Europeans expect of individuals in these positions.

Although Americans are informal, they do react strongly to being corrected or reprimanded in public. They prefer that this be done in private, if at all. The German propensity toward correcting strangers is shocking and offensive to most Americans.

There are a number of paradoxes in the American character that puzzle foreigners. For instance, hand in hand with their individualism is a competing drive to conform. Despite the surface appearance of easy informality, egalitarianism, and great freedom, there are very strong pressures to conform in certain areas of American culture. The rules are not always explicit but they do exist, and, as in every culture, social pressure reinforces conformity.

Appearances are important to Americans, both personal appearance and the outside appearance of their homes, especially in middle-class suburbs. Neighbors become very upset if property is not well maintained and cared for. They think indifference to the appearance of one's house implies an anti-social attitude and a lack of concern for one's neighbors, not to mention the fear that unsightliness may also bring down property values. Americans become disturbed when neighbors don't cut the grass, shovel the snow on the sidewalk or driveway, or attend to outside painting and repairs.

There is also strong pressure on Americans to be team players, to go along with the majority. In business, this means not rocking the boat or making waves, and in politics it all too often means supporting a leader at the expense of telling the truth or of doing the right thing. The pressure to get along well with others means individualism is less appreciated than conformity on the job.

Approval and popularity are strong motivators for Americans, who have a deep need to be accepted and liked. There are numerous books on how to make friends and how to persuade people to accept your thinking. The American drive to be liked, accepted, and approved of by a wide circle of friends and associates means they must inevitably sacrifice some of their individuality. The French are less likely to hide their real selves and hence the French are equally less likely to be good team players in business or elsewhere.

Another of the great paradoxes in American culture is the conflict between the individual's drive for acceptance and popularity and the drive for success and achievement. People who value getting ahead in a career more than getting along with others often find themselves isolated (American women particularly face this problem when they enter fields heretofore reserved for men). They may be admired but not generally liked.

However strong the American need to conform and to be a team player, the American's first loyalty is still to self, family, and career, not the company. In order to advance in salary or rank, the individual may move from one company to another. A person may work for many different companies in one lifetime. This is normal and accepted in American business and is not considered an indication of disloyalty and unreliability.

Americans also have little personal loyalty in their business dealings. Being pragmatic, they do business where they "get the best deal," which usually means the best price. In their personal life, individuals often prefer to do business with someone they know is reliable, whom they've dealt with for years. Their personal relationship overrides their desire for the lowest price.

American friendship depends more on common interests and congeniality than on shared philosophical beliefs. In contrast to people from other cultures, Americans maintain friendships with people of differing philosophies and beliefs. Another difference is that American friends do not always discuss deep personal problems with each other; often they go to professionals for counseling instead. However, friends are important to Americans and despite the mobility that characterizes the society, they do form some deep, lasting relationships. Some even maintain links with childhood friends, including classmates from school and college.

Keeping up the standard of living in the United States leaves most people with little money for savings. While Americans are not traditionally savers, many families do save money to pay for their children's education. Since higher education in the U.S. is expensive compared to Europe, this leaves little for other needs in the future. Nevertheless, Americans can be extraordinarily generous to others. They contribute billions of dollars to charity each year (nearly $90 billion in recent years) and are easily moved to respond to the misfortunes of others, both at home and abroad. This generosity is matched by no other country we know. Business leaders are among the many Americans who spend a great deal of time and money on charitable and civic activities. As one American banker said, "The sense of altruism and its concomitant commitment of time runs through all levels of U.S. industry."

Many Americans are involved in civic and community affairs or are active in political parties at the local, state, and national level. Others work in organizations such as the League of Women Voters, dedicated to informing the public about elections and candidates running for office, as well as in groups concerned with environmental issues and social problems. Most communities abound in civic organizations. In addition, many families belong to churches with programs for social welfare to which they devote considerable time.

AMERICAN BUSINESS

The Role of Business: Generator of Wealth

The United States is the least socialistic of the major modern industrial countries. According to a recent study published by the International Monetary Fund, more than 95 percent of the American economy is run by private enterprise, and only a small percent of capital formation in the United States is supported by government funding. Most American telephone, telegraph, television, radio, electric, and transportation systems are privately owned.

Unlike their counterparts in France, the top graduates of leading universities in the United States do not usually enter government service; instead they choose business or the professions. American business attracts talent and ability because it pays well, and, in the U.S., talent goes where the rewards are. Later in their careers some executives may spend a few years in key government positions in Washington, but, with a few exceptions, government service as a career cannot compete with private industry.

Most Americans regard business as a positive force in society and are well aware that the country's financial well-being depends on a healthy economy. The recession in the early 1980s brought the first widespread unemployment in the U.S. since the 1930s, making Americans aware that business affects

THE AMERICANS

every aspect of society. In a recession, everyone suffers, not just
the unemployed, as the ripple effect engulfs the entire country.
American business is very concerned about its corporate image
and spends millions of dollars telling the American public about
the contributions it makes to American society as well as about
its products. (This concept of corporate image is absent in
Germany and other European countries.) American business
doesn't just provide jobs and pay taxes; it also supports thousands of civic and cultural programs. American schools and
universities receive critical funding from business (currently
over $1.6 billion a year). Public television also has many
business-sponsored programs, including high-quality docu-
mentaries and musical programs, presented as a public service
with few product commercials. Business support for education
and cultural programs is not found in either Germany or France,
where the government provides the support.

Large Corporations, Mergers, and Takeovers

American business today is dominated by large corporations.
Recently, of the 104 million working Americans, half worked in
firms of more than 500 employees, and one-third of these were
in firms of more than 5,000 employees. Within large companies
there is a growing trend toward decentralization to counteract
the overwhelming size of many business firms. Some companies limit the size of divisions within a company, thereby
creating more opportunities for individual initiative and foster-
ing closer identification with the company.

One new development in American business that is causing
much justified concern is the expanding number of corporate
mergers and takeovers. In 1988 there were 3,637 corporate
mergers, totaling 311.4 billion dollars—up 41.6% from 1987.
The work force of a company targeted for a takeover is usually
drastically reduced at all levels, leaving many people suddenly
jobless (between 1982 and 1985, 800,000 managers were laid
off). Because of mergers and takeovers, the number of compa-

155

nies within a given industry declines. Indeed, in some American industries there are only a few companies left, and such a situation diminishes the industry's creativity and the variety of its resources, both human and otherwise.

One big problem in American business is identifying the complex of factors that creates a successful enterprise. Unfortunately, the drive to "rationalize" management and to make management "scientific" sometimes destroys the human foundation on which business success has been built.

In general it is the rare manager who really knows why one thing succeeds and another fails, why one market strategy works and another does not. Most American business executives are highly specialized and narrow in their focus, but there are exceptional people who lead and innovate (such as the late Alfred Sloan of General Motors). Reasons for their success are rarely understood by those who follow.

Current Challenges to American Business

American business today is challenged by constantly changing conditions in technology, world markets, overall economic situations, the weak dollar, ever increasing bureaucracies, demands to make businesses more responsive to human needs, and foreign competition. In 1988, for the third consecutive year, West Germany exported more than any other country ($323.3 billion, compared to the United States' $321.6 billion). This figure is all the more startling considering West Germany's population of 60.8 million, compared to a population of 250 million in the United States. The U.S. remains the world's largest importer, more than West Germany and France combined, but its real cause for concern is its trade deficit, which topped $137.9 billion in 1988.

Another challenge that American business must face is that of educating its workers. Many American high school graduates are unable to read and follow simple directions or perform basic mathematical tasks. Business has begun to respond by giving money to public and trade schools and universities. But education takes time, and in the interim many businesses are forced to hire employees poorly prepared to function in a work environment. Some corporations have developed in-house, remedial training programs, including courses in reading, writing, and computation. In a society where high tech innovations appear in the office and on the assembly line with great frequency, there is no place for people who lack basic skills.

To be attractive to investors, especially the large institutional investors that dominate the market, companies need to have a consistent record of regular increases in earnings. Many observers think this is one factor in the short-term demands of investors. Such corporate goals as capital investment in new equipment, research and development, and training for employees, for example, may well be deferred or never achieved because of the pressure on management to show good results each quarter and each year. Certainly, poor earnings in a quarter or a year adversely affect the value of a company's stock.

In the years since World War II, American management has become obsessed with the bottom line. In the words of one automobile executive, "The bean counters took over." Disregarding the need for long-term planning, American business has concentrated on cost control and short-term profits. In several major industries, research and development and capital expenditures for new plants and for new technologies have been minimal; this is particularly true of the steel and automobile industries, and their decline has adversely affected hundreds of other industries. Detroit automobile executives ignored the advice of their own designers and engineers, who urged modernization of factories, introduction of innovations such as front-wheel drive, concentration on energy-efficient cars, and quality control. As a consequence, when world oil prices rose, Detroit was unprepared; it had nothing to compete with the small cars from Europe and Japan (see David Halberstam's *The Reckoning*).

The uneven quality of American goods is another handicap in international markets and there are many complaints from businesspeople and customers in countries such as Germany and in Japan where poor quality is unacceptable. Coupled with quality control problems are a lack of adequate parts and poor after-sales service, which are basic requirements in an international market. Once a company loses its reputation for reliability, it can take years to regain it and no amount of advertising hype will overcome a poor performance record.

> For the most part, Americans regard their company objectively, as a vehicle by which one gains power, self-satisfaction, professional stimuli, and income. It is a means to an end.
>
> —American banker

There are some American employees who feel great loyalty toward their company. Most employees, however, are primarily concerned about their own careers and expect to change jobs and companies if it enhances their opportunities for greater pay, greater recognition, or promotion. Changing jobs is often the only route to advancement. As noted earlier, no stigma is attached to moving from one company to another; it is accepted from the executive level to the factory. There are many job placement firms ("head hunters") which specialize in helping people find new and better jobs.

Employee mobility has many ramifications, not the least of which is that decisions are often made on short-term considerations. Employees who think they will not be with the company for very long are less concerned about decisions that will not have an impact until some future time when they may no longer be there. Thus, mobility is one more contributor to the short-term orientation of American business.

Loyalty is adversely affected by recessions that necessitate reductions in personnel, by business failures, and, as noted earlier, most recently by corporate mergers and takeovers which increase in number each year and often lead to mass firings. Is it any wonder that employees' first loyalties are to themselves and their families?

Another factor that influences employee loyalty is aspiration to advancement, which is not always possible within one particular company. Loyalty to one company is also undercut by the problems facing two-career families, where both husband and wife work. If one is transferred to another city, the other must often leave to follow the spouse.

Being fired is not uncommon in American business nor is it considered a death sentence to one's career. Many successful American executives have been dismissed at some point in their careers. Lee Iacocca is a well-known example, who, after being dismissed from the presidency of Ford Motor Company, went on to achieve success at Chrysler albeit with government assistance.

How Business Works

American business is strongly influenced by American culture. Three key characteristics of the best American businesses are

1. clear lines of authority,

2. detailed instructions for subordinates, and

3. constant feedback on individual performance.

The first question an American employee asks is, "Whom do I report to?" The employee's immediate bosses are the people who tell them what to do and how to do it and evaluate their on-the-job performance with frequent written reports. For Americans, feedback and evaluation are a life-long process, starting at the lowest levels in school and continuing through the university—by which time students are often more preoccupied with grades than with what they learn. Americans' need for evaluation is tied to their deep need for praise and encouragement.

In most medium- and large-size companies employees expect to receive a job description that defines their responsibilities, scope of authority, and sometimes the specific tasks to be done. Close supervision is common and expected. However, employees may also be expected to, on occasion, demonstrate initiative.

For motivating employees American business has discovered that special awards and recognition ceremonies are helpful. Most American firms have achievement programs with elaborate rituals for presenting awards which employees can proudly display on their office walls. When they do not receive individual feedback, American employees often become anxious and unsure of themselves.

Though Americans seem to have a relaxed and informal working environment, it's important to remember that there are rules and regulations—and lines of authority—even though these rules are seldom spelled out. Even if employees call the boss by her or his first name, the boss has plenty of power—and both employer and employees know it.

For an insightful guide to behavior in American business, we recommend *Letitia Baldrige's Complete Guide to Executive Manners*. Baldrige maintains that good manners based on consideration for others constitutes good business, and her book covers a wide variety of situations with practical advice (see reading list).

> It's hard to communicate directly to top American executives because they're so isolated by their staff.
>
> —German executive in the steel industry

The management of many American companies is top-down, highly compartmentalized, and linear. However, there is a small but growing trend toward information-based organizations which emphasize shared information and decentralized control (see Peter Drucker's article, "Playing in the Information-Based Orchestra," in the reading list). In general, however, Americans in business resist sharing information; some refuse entirely. Most Americans, on the other hand, do require detailed information and guidance. We warn foreigners, "Don't assume Americans are well informed; often they are not."

In American business there are informal but important information networks within the company. Information is gathered and disbursed at the water cooler, at lunch, at meals in the executive dining room, on company trips, on the golf course, and during after-hours socializing. Maintaining one's information networks is a vital part of one's job. Yet, Americans remain quite compartmentalized in their thinking and organizational patterns.

In meetings Americans are impatient and want to get down to business immediately, in striking contrast to the French, who prefer to build personal relationships first. This impatience is related to the American tempo; sometimes it may reflect an absence of manners. In general, however, most Americans have been taught that it's best to come to the point quickly and to avoid ambiguity. As noted, they basically distrust indirection and skirting an issue. They think it's an attempt to hide something. Obviously, such an approach creates problems for Americans interacting with people such as the French and the Japanese.

Written communication is very important in American business. Most firms have regular channels of written communication to keep employees informed of events and changes related to their jobs. There are also monthly or even weekly reports and many interoffice memos. Because Americans are procedures-oriented, there is usually a steady flow of paper outlining exactly what is to be done. Foreigners who work with Americans have to learn to write memos, reports, and evaluations. Paperwork is always important in low-context cultures, where compartmentalization blocks the free flow of information.

Planning and Scheduling

The American custom of short-term planning in business is an excellent illustration of the hidden power of culture and how it affects business. As mentioned earlier, America's business planning intervals are considerably shorter than those of its major trading partners. In part because of the need for quarterly financial reporting, American business is preoccupied with immediate performance and accustomed to thinking in short-term intervals, which has proved to be a tremendous handicap in competing in the international market, especially with coun-

161

tries such as Germany and Japan, where businesses plan for twenty, thirty, even fifty years in the future. The cost to the United States is billions of dollars annually and will continue until American business understands the price it pays for short-term thinking and planning (see Edward T. Hall's *The Dance of Life* for a more detailed study of this topic).

Most American executives have their time scheduled for months in advance, and, since many of them travel extensively, lead time is very important in arranging appointments. Americans like meetings and appointments to be arranged well in advance—several weeks to several months depending on the number and the importance of the people involved. Last-minute requests by telephone are considered an inconvenience and may even be interpreted as an insult; the implication is that the person making the request is more important than the person who must change his or her schedule. Prior commitments make last-minute changes difficult for most executives. The amount of lead time for various business activities in the United States varies with the importance of the individual as well as the regional time system. For example, when we were arranging interviews with American executives in California and New York, we noticed a significant difference in the elapsed time before a response was received from these two areas. We wrote to everyone two months ahead of time to arrange appointments. The response from California was usually by letter, two weeks or more after our letter was received. Even then, some executives stated they were not sure of their schedule a month in advance. In contrast the response from New York was immediate, usually by telephone, confirming appointments six to eight weeks ahead. Each region has its own time system, which should be taken into account.

Meetings: The Importance of Agendas

American meetings usually include the boss and her or his subordinates, who are often equally ranked heads of units in the

162

organization and who report directly to the boss. Meetings generally do not cut across hierarchical levels; those decision makers in attendance are usually of similar rank.

Most American meetings follow an agenda, prepared for the top-ranking person at the meeting and sometimes circulated ahead of time. Topics for discussion should be listed on the agenda before the meeting begins. Americans do not always discuss the agenda informally ahead of time, and there may or may not be advance work on consensus.

Americans take an informal, relaxed attitude about many business meetings, saying in effect, "Let's agree on the principles and work out the details later." Meetings are held for many different reasons: to discuss and reach decisions among those present, to brief the staff or to alert employees to changes in policy or future plans, to discuss sales or personnel issues, to meet with advertising agencies or with distributors or suppliers, or to draw up procedures. At times meetings can become quite heated as various points of view are discussed and debated. There may well be confrontations and disagreements that must be resolved.

Participants in meetings who have something to contribute or who want a decision made must be sure to get it on the agenda ahead of time. They should bring all their facts and figures and practice their verbal presentation beforehand. It's often a good idea for the person presenting to have a written digest of major points (short and easy to understand) which can be circulated at the meeting. Most American meetings are not pro forma; the purpose is not to give formal approval to decisions already made.

Americans tend to be aggressive and articulate in meetings and are impressed by forceful presentations amply buttressed by data. Americans will sometimes deliberately adopt a confrontational stance in hopes of intimidating others. Foreigners who are not as articulate or whose style is less aggressive may feel excluded in American meetings. Americans in turn need to be aware of differences in communication styles and allow foreign participants more time in which to communicate; and, most

163

important, Americans should listen very carefully to what the foreigner is saying.

Everyone agrees that Americans have too many meetings. A 1987 survey by executive recruiting firm Heidrick & Struggles, Inc., revealed that the average American executive spends 17.3 hours a week in meetings plus an additional 6.3 hours in preparation. In other words, the average CEO spends a third of her or his time in or on meetings.

Successful Managers

Top American executives are usually selected for their ability to make decisions and take responsibility. They are then given authority and expected to act. Managers are expected to follow procedures, handle their own problems, not make waves, and be good team players. Business executives who are most admired are the dynamic leaders who drive themselves and others to get results; in this they are not unlike German managers.

Charles Garfield has identified the characteristics of effective managers in American business (see reading list). He reports that these characteristics include transcending previous performance, avoiding becoming too comfortable in the job, enjoying the art of their work, rehearsing coming events in their minds, avoiding placing blame, and examining the worst consequences of a situation under consideration (the so-called "worst-case scenario") before making a decision.

How different some of these American management practices are from those of the Germans and the French! German managers insist on following established procedures exactly; they use written communication and hold their employees responsible for performance, but they do not supervise them. They expect their employees to solve their own problems. French managers exert strong control over subordinates and decision making is highly centralized. Their style is autocratic: they expect obedience from everyone. Most important, French managers tend to share information only with people of equal status in their own network, not with employees. Successful American managers usually share information much more freely and have a much less autocratic style.

Women in Business

Today many American women hold positions of responsibility and authority in business. This is the result of the women's rights movement and women's fight for fair employment laws, which guard against job discrimination and require that promotions be made on merit. Many American businesses actively recruit women and encourage them to apply for managerial positions. However, there are still problems for American women in business. We refer the reader to an excellent book by Hennig and Jardim, *The Managerial Woman* (see reading list).

One of the critical problems women face is that they do not have access to many of the crucial power networks within their own companies. Often these networks are closed because their male members have been working together for years and are not receptive to newcomers. As a result, women have had to build networks of their own, which takes years while people get to know and trust each other and learn who can best help them. Women may also need to find a mentor who can help them build a track record and lend them credibility before they are taken seriously by their male peers.

A 1986 *Wall Street Journal* report on the corporate woman (see "The Glass Ceiling" by Hymowitz and Schellhardt in the reading list) presents a review of the barriers American women face in business today. Women are blocked from promotion to top corporate jobs, usually for the following reasons:

> Many top male executives (especially older males) are uncomfortable with female executives and deliberately keep them out of the boardroom. Male executives also tend to make promotion decisions based on a colleague's abilities on the golf course or the racquetball court, thereby

165

automatically excluding women from being considered for top jobs.

• Women with children must often interrupt their careers temporarily, and this break in work is held against them.

• Many women must move from one city and job to another because of their husbands' job transfers, thus diverting their own career progress.

• Most American women are forced to hold two full-time jobs: one in an office and one at home, where they get little or no assistance. This situation leads to stress and fatigue (the "Superwoman Syndrome"). Women with young children face even greater difficulties in finding adequate child care. Most European countries offer government-funded day care centers, but the U.S. government, despite lip service to the idea of supporting strong families, has only recently begun to make such a commitment to aid American families.

The most important problem for women continues to be salary. The vast majority of American women still earn much less money than do men in exactly the same or comparable positions.

Labor in Transition

Thirty years ago, one-third of the work force in the United States were members of labor unions. By 1988 that number had dropped to 17 percent. The sharpest declines have been in the United Mine Workers of America and the United Steelworkers of America, both industries that have been severely handicapped by obsolete technology, high wages, and overwhelming competition from abroad. This same competition has also affected union composition in the textile and garment industries.

American industry today suffers from the weakness of the U.S. dollar, which has led to a large world trade deficit coupled with a huge federal domestic deficit. Many American products are no longer competitive in world markets, which has also had a negative effect on labor unions. Another factor that has contributed to the downtrend in the strength of American labor is badly planned government deregulation of the airline, trucking, and communication industries. While old companies are breaking up and being recreated in new forms, unions must wait before pressing demands on new companies; also, the new management that comes in after mergers and acquisitions have taken place may be hostile to organized labor and has in some cases taken steps to destroy it.

American labor unions are now in a state of transition as they face the problems of lower productivity, foreign competition, and the overall decline of many segments of American industry. At present, unions are concentrating on several new goals: guaranteed jobs, with the proviso that if one job is abolished another will be found for the worker within the company; greater flexibility in wage demands and work regulations, including allowing workers to perform several different tasks and encouraging worker participation in decision making; and improvements in quality control to compete with foreign competition. Labor unions in the U.S. must also reorient themselves away from heavy industry and "male only" exclusionary policies in the management of unions and recognize that their largest untapped strength is the "pink-collar ghetto" of low-paying jobs filled by female clerical and service workers.

Foreign companies in the U.S. will need to be aware of the strict laws affecting labor and working conditions, both federal and state. The advice of experts in the field of labor may be necessary.

Public Relations, Corporate Image, and Advertising

In the United States there is a difference between a person's facade and her or his image. Facade is what people present as their public exterior; it's composed of their personality and their personification of cultural values. Image is artificial and imposed

167

and is, in business, the product of public relations and advertising. The image can be a product image, a corporate image, or the image of the company's top official. Many American companies are closely identified in the public mind with the person who runs the company, such as Lee Iacocca with Chrysler and Mary Kay Ash with Mary Kay Cosmetics. The product, the corporation, and the CEO should all project a consistent image, and this is the job of the company's advertising agency.

Americans are very image-conscious. They think in terms of how their actions will affect their own personal image, the image of their product, or the image of their company. When Americans have to make a decision, they consider how the decision will make them or their company look. The American preoccupation with image leads some foreigners to decry the shallowness of Americans.

Corporate reputation can be the determining factor in public acceptance of a product if the product is similar in quality and price to a competitor's. Dependability, performance, quality, and price are all part of a company's image. Sales in a competitive market are directly affected by how well a company communicates its image of dependability and high quality to the public at large.

The American communication style is like a newspaper headline: short and to the point. Americans prefer digests to long articles and detailed reports. They often announce at the beginning of oral presentations what they are going to talk about and when the discourse will end. Short, punchy presentations with humor are preferred (except, perhaps, for technical, scientific, or academic papers). In the U.S., starting a speech with a joke is common, but it would be a major mistake in West Germany. Conversely, beginning a speech with a presentation of the historical background of an issue—which is done frequently by German speakers—would bore an American audience to tears. Because many Americans have a narrow professional focus, they are not interested in general or background information, but just in what they need to know right then. Germans want lots of background information, historical context, and examples. The French, of course, prefer elegant, elaborate presentations that display wit and savoir-faire.

As we discussed in parts 2 and 3, the function of German advertising is to transmit information while French advertising works to release a positive emotional response. The function of American advertising is to hype the product.

As we have noted, Americans often exaggerate in both their written and their oral communication. This is particularly true in advertising, which is based on hyperbole, or "hype." Although ads in the United States may contain information, it is seldom detailed and is usually a bolster for the claims of product superiority. Exaggerated claims that a product is the best, newest, most fashionable, or finest are effective in the U.S. but would be both offensive and illegal in West Germany and would win no awards in France.

Most of the money spent on advertising in the United States goes to print ads. Local advertisers all over the country spend millions for newspaper ads in their own areas, from very small ones in weekly hometown newspapers to full-page ads in the *New York Times*. Because of the complexity of the American market, a lot of money is spent annually to analyze and conduct market surveys so that advertisers can target their ads for a specific group. In the U.S. the CEO often takes a personal interest in a company's image and advertising; American ad agencies are thus accustomed to working with the CEO and do not feel secure unless the CEO is involved. This is not true in Europe, where the advertising department of a company is usually the only group handling advertisements.

Americans like idealized images. The women in them are usually young, healthy, and beautiful, and the men are young, strong, and handsome. Children are clean and smiling. Even ads directed toward older population groups show young-looking though gray-haired people.

U.S. markets are segmented not only by age, gender, and income but also by region and ethnicity. There are fast-growing ethnic groups who will exert a tremendous economic influence in the future, such as the American Hispanic population (there are now over 250,000 Spanish-owned businesses).

The importance of getting to know local and regional customs and buying habits in the United States was emphasized to us by a European advertising executive: "Marketing, selling, distributing, and advertising have to be in the hands of local people. You can't just come in and say, 'Do it my way.'" Another advertising executive addressed the same point: "You must be very French in France, very German in Germany, and very American in America."

Characteristics of Successful American Business Executives

The kinds of people who succeed in business in the United States are goal-oriented, concerned with individual achievement, and interested in the development of their own careers. They also tend to be pragmatic, assertive, and relatively egalitarian; at the same time they need constant feedback, evaluations, praise, and rewards—something they would not get in German or French business. Unlike business in France or West Germany, there are powerful American executives who are very young; Europeans favor older, more seasoned top executives. Women are found at top levels in some American businesses but are rare in Western Europe.

Decision making in American business is usually "top-down"— which means American executives often make decisions without consulting subordinates. The result is that decisions are often made without crucial input from various levels within the organization. In a compartmentalized business organization it is very difficult to get vital information to the decision makers. This is certainly true in Germany and to a lesser degree in the U.S.

Many American businesspeople are driven to compete for promotion and will sometimes sacrifice social and family life to work, a situation rare in West Germany and France, where weekends and holidays are sacred and work is not always the dominant force in one's daily life.

170

Corporate Culture and Local Culture

In their excellent book *Corporate Cultures,* Terrence Deal and Allan Kennedy point out that businesses which have strong corporate cultures have certain advantages over those that don't. A strong corporate culture provides shared ideals and a common way of communicating. It also performs several other important functions:

1. Increasing context (i.e., providing necessary background data)

2. Decreasing compartmentalization

3. Increasing information flow

4. Facilitating organizational unification and coordination

5. Increasing survival capabilities

In good times a strong corporate culture is not a prerequisite to survival. In bad times it is vital. Companies that do not have a strong corporate culture and a strong corporate image will tend to fragment under the stress of the struggle to survive when times become difficult. Strong corporate cultures are cohesive; they bind their employees together. They encourage cooperation and enable companies to respond quickly and effectively to changing conditions.

But a strong corporate culture at home does not necessarily guarantee an effective corporate presence abroad. Overseas, it is necessary first to create an environment in which the indigenous employees can flourish. Management must adapt the company's corporate culture to the local culture. This adaptation requires great patience in the home office and depends in large part on the selection of the foreign manager, who must understand the requirements of the home office and also have the skills to interact effectively with the local people. Interfacing between the home office and the local affiliate is the greatest challenge to any overseas population. In time local employees should be encouraged to adapt the corporate culture and corporate image to ensure maximum impact on both local people and local markets.

American Business Executives Abroad

Corporate cultures are apparently more exportable than national cultures and are certainly more understandable to Americans, who are used to the idea that working for a company means doing things the company way.

When Americans work overseas, they tend to isolate themselves in "golden ghettos" and interact with each other rather than with the people of the host country. We have observed this phenomenon for over thirty years; only in the last decade have we noted a heartening change. Today many Americans, the younger executives in particular, really do try to live in the country of assignment, making friends and learning the language. Some have had prior experience living abroad with their parents or in the Peace Corps. This change in attitude and behavior has made an enormous difference in their ability to adapt and learn the foreign culture.

American business is often criticized for its lack of concern for the families of its overseas employees. Many executives are assigned overseas for short periods, usually two years, which is simply not enough time to learn the language and integrate into the society. Additionally, since they expect to be leaving in two years, they may feel the effort of learning the language would be wasted, another example of how the American short-term time orientation adversely affects business performance.

Spouses of American executives overseas bear the brunt of adjusting to the local culture since they must cope with housing, schools, shopping, repairs, health care, and social life. They need not only language training but orientation to the culture as well. Quite often American spouses are unable to obtain work permits. With their husbands or wives working long hours or traveling extensively and the children at school, the spouses are left alone with no means of communication—with predictable results. The rate of marital difficulties, divorce, and alcoholism among American families abroad is high and reflects a lack of understanding and intelligent planning by American business. Recently, however, some American business firms have become slightly more realistic and are now willing to make longer assignments overseas, permitting employee and spouse to become fluent in both language and culture.

American overseas business personnel today are much better educated and informed than their predecessors of thirty years ago and more competent and adaptable. For many years American business was not cognizant of the crucial importance of proper selection and training of overseas personnel. As a result they lost millions of dollars. In the past there was an unfortunate tendency to transfer problem employees abroad, and even today there are many Americans working overseas who should never have left the United States. You can usually spot them in restaurants and bars of clubs or international hotels, loudly voicing their frustrations with locals, arrogant and impatient. Despite these unfortunate errors in selection, there has been a noticeable improvement in the quality of American business representation overseas. An executive who has been successful in the U.S. often has difficulty when transferred abroad because of her or his expectations of continued success. When those expectations are not met (because the techniques that were successful in the U.S. do not always work in foreign cultures), the result can be a devastating sense of failure. The ability to cope with failure is therefore a prime qualification for cross-cultural effectiveness, but is unfortunately not a quality highly prized in American business.

It is our strong recommendation that only the best and most adaptable people be sent overseas and that their training in both language and cross-cultural effectiveness be extensive. A recent study for the Southern Governors' Association concluded, "We have yet to learn a critical lesson: the language of trade is the language of the customer." We would add that the language of the customer includes not only the spoken language but also the language of behavior, that is, the culture.

Once the company has invested the time and money in training, it should leave the employees in the country long enough to reap the benefits (a minimum of five years). Several executives agreed with the highly experienced general manager of a German subsidiary, who said, "American companies make a big mistake by rotating their managers too often."

Companies should also develop long-term plans for utilizing the expertise of overseas employees once they return to headquarters. All too often their knowledge and experience is ignored and lost. Even worse, their overseas experience may be a handicap to career advancement in the United States since they may be perceived as having been out of the mainstream.

In our interviews overseas, almost all the directors of American companies overseas ranked the home office as their number one problem. Americans have a world-wide reputation for oversupervising their foreign operations. One top manager (a Swiss) with many years of experience working for American companies abroad had this to say: "American companies tend to keep you on a short leash. There are constant demands for reports and financial data. At headquarters you are smothered with staff who 'know better' about everything. Overseas you are alone but you are closely watched; whenever there's a blip, you hear from headquarters and they hover and hover."

It is difficult for headquarters to understand what is happening in a foreign operation. The people who are most likely to know are those on the spot who are cognizant of the cultural differences involved. Thus, the best policy for the executives at the home office is to assign good people to foreign posts and then *listen to what they say.*

Key Points for Foreigners to Keep in Mind

There are several characteristics that flow from the massive size of the United States as well as from the great variety of cultural antecedents that distinguish American culture from all others.

174

In spite of the numerous and visible inequities in the American system, there is still no society in the world that provides both the freedom and the opportunity to become a success for anyone who has brains or talent and is willing to apply her- or himself. America is still the land of opportunity.

Because of the way in which American business and marketing systems are organized, and possibly because of reinforcement from the extensive and ubiquitous television commercial, the tempo of American business interactions is unusually fast. Everything is faster and bigger in the United States. Keep this in mind: Americans tend to "tailgate" other people.

In the U.S., there is no defined class system. People are constantly moving up and down in the social system because of variations in their financial and educational status. Americans are very status-conscious and place great emphasis on status symbols such as money, celebrity, power, image, possessions, and institutional affiliations.

In over a quarter of a century of working with, talking to, interviewing, and being friends with people from other parts of the world, there is one point that is made consistently: American friendship patterns are of the temporary sort and often do not go very deep. The reasons behind this are many and varied and relate to the unusual mobility of most Americans, especially those in business.

As a consequence of their extreme individualism, American loyalties are for the most part linked to careers and *not* to the organization. Loyalty to organizations is discouraged by the narrow, bottom-line, cost-cutting philosophy of many American business firms.

When Working with American Business

1. Remember that American business works in a short time frame. Its executives and managers want immediate results and are not as interested in building long-term relationships as Europeans are.

175

2. In general, when you employ Americans, check their education and previous employment references carefully. Do not assume everyone is honest. In our research, we heard many complaints about falsified records.

3. Be very careful in choosing an American manager. Spend the necessary time and money to investigate the backgrounds of those you consider good candidates. Encourage the person you select to make friends and build networks at your home office.

4. Americans arrive at meetings with an agenda they wish to follow. If you want something discussed, be sure it is placed on the agenda ahead of time. Bring a short written statement to circulate.

5. Be prepared for the problems of compartmentalization in American business. Do not assume information will be shared.

When Working with Individual Americans

1. Because the United States is a mix of many ethnic groups, you must determine whether the person you are dealing with is monochronic or polychronic so that you can then adjust your strategy accordingly. Most Americans are monochronic: they do one thing at a time, they don't like interruptions, and they have a strong need to finish whatever they are working on. They also compartmentalize information and do not share it freely. Even members of minority ethnic groups tend to adopt the monochronic behaviors of the majority culture in their business dealings.

2. Americans are individually oriented and concerned with their own careers. Their loyalty is first to themselves and then to their employer or organization.

3. Americans want to be liked and accepted. They prefer people who don't make waves and are good team players.

4. Equality and egalitarianism are important to Americans. They resent people who pull rank or seem to consider themselves superior.

5. Most Americans are open, friendly, casual, and informal in their manners. They do not mean to insult you if they call you by your first name.

6. Americans like to come right to the point. They are uncomfortable with indirection and subtlety.

7. Learn all about the Americans you work with: their background, education, and hobbies.

8. Keep in mind that appearances are important to Americans.

9. Be open to diversity.

10. When dealing with American employees, give specific (preferably written) instructions, avoid vagueness and indirection, be lavish with praise and recognition, and do not discriminate against or disparage anyone, especially women and minorities. If you need to correct an American employee, first seek guidance from your American staff. To be effective, correction of a subordinate must be based on knowledge of that person.

Summary

Remember that culture is many things, but it is primarily a system for creating, sending, storing, and processing information. Here is a summary of some of the conceptual tools we have provided to guide you, five keys to help you unlock the doors to a foreign country: time, context, space, information flow, and interfacing.

Time

Time is one of the fundamental bases on which all cultures rest and around which all activities revolve. Understanding the difference between monochronic time and polychronic time is essential to success in international business. The American working in a foreign country must immediately determine whether the people are monochronic or polychronic because this will affect *everything:* how business is organized, whether schedules are adhered to, how much lead time is needed, and the basic orientation of the culture—past, present, or future. Pay particular attention to the matter of schedules and agendas and whether or not they are followed. It's important to learn how to get your items on their agenda, but it's just as important to allow them to get their items on your agenda.

For a discussion of time as it is perceived in different parts of the world, see *The Dance of Life* by Edward T. Hall.

Context

High-context people are well informed and maintain extensive information networks to insure their being abreast of the latest developments; they require a minimum of background information; and they are accustomed to many interruptions and cannot always adhere to schedule. Low-context people are not well informed outside their own special area of expertise. They are compartmentalized and require lots of background information before they can make a decision. They can suffer from information overload if their channels become filled with too many messages (memos, procedures, instructions, requests for data, etc.). This overload breaks their action chain and they fall behind.

For further information about high- and low-context people and action chains, we refer the reader to Edward T. Hall's *Beyond Culture.*

Space

Space, like time, is a core system in all cultures. Everything is organized in space, and spatial organization can be the key to unlocking the mentality of the people.

People like the Germans are highly territorial; they barricade themselves behind heavy doors and soundproof walls to try to seal themselves off from others in order to concentrate on their work. The French have a close personal distance and are not as territorial. They are tied to people and thrive on constant interaction and high-information flow to provide them the context they need.

Edward T. Hall has examined how different cultures use space in the book *The Hidden Dimension.*

Information Flow

How information is handled in different cultures is one of the most important things to know about any culture. In polychronic countries such as France, information flows freely within the peer group, moving rapidly as if it had a life of its own, but is very restricted between groups. In monochronic countries such as Germany, information flows slowly, delayed by rigid compartmentalization.

Interfacing

Some cultures are easier to interface with than others, and business strategies will differ accordingly. The greater the cultural difference in such things as time, context, and space, the more difficult the interface will be.

Cultural interfacing follows five basic principles:

1. The higher the context of either the culture of the industry, the more difficult the interface;

2. The greater the complexity of the elements, the more difficult the interface;

3. The greater the cultural distance, the more difficult the interface;

4. The greater the number of levels in the system, the more difficult the interface;

5. Very simple, low-context, highly evolved, mechanical systems tend to produce fewer interface problems than multiple-level systems of great complexity that depend on human talent for their success.

Culture's Building Blocks: The Organizing Frames

The basic organizing frames we have provided will enable you to build on your own knowledge and experience in a foreign culture and begin to see for yourself the underlying structure of that culture. You will also be able to integrate your experiences in a way that is meaningful for you. Once you have mastered a few basic concepts, you will find yourself better equipped to handle day-to-day working situations. A knowledge of the culture plus the language will make a great difference in your success as well as your enjoyment of the experience of working and living abroad.

Remember it is more important to release the right responses in others than it is to send what you think are the right messages.

Glossary

Action chain

An *action chain,* a term borrowed from ethology, is a fixed sequence of events in which people alternately release appropriate responses in each other in order to achieve an agreed-upon or predictable goal. The steps or links in the chain are culturally determined and vary from culture to culture. Examples of action chains include courtship, getting married, completing a sale, conducting complex political negotiations, and setting up a business.

Culture

Culture is a technical term used by anthropologists to refer to a system for creating, sending, storing, and processing information developed by human beings, which differentiates them from other life forms. The terms *mores, tradition, custom,* and *habit* are subsumed under the cultural umbrella. Sometimes *culture* is used in reference to the fine arts. While art and literature do indeed form an important part of a culture, in this book the term is used in its wider context.

High Context and Low Context

These terms refer to the fact that when people communicate, they take for granted how much the listener knows about the subject under discussion. In *low-context* communication, the listener knows very little and must be told practically everything. In *high-context* communication the listener is already "contexted" and so does not need to be given much background information. An extreme example: twins who have shared a long life in proximity to each other work at a much higher level on the context scale than do people of different cultures who have only just met.

Interfacing

The term *interfacing* derives from the technical terminology of computers. Computers are modeled after the human brain and have some similarities to cultures in the way they are organized and work. Creating the proper interface is nothing more than creating a system for translating the messages of one part of the computer or program to another; it is the key to combining and using different systems. Overcoming the difficulties inherent in interfacing between such contradictory systems as monochronic and polychronic time requires conscious effort and much goodwill before relationships begin to work as expected.

Monochronic and Polychronic Cultures

Monochronic cultures are those in which the time base is an outgrowth of the industrial revolution. Monochronic cultures stress a high degree of scheduling, concentration on one thing at a time (hence the name), and an elaborate code of behavior built around promptness in meeting obligations and appointments. *Polychronic* cultures are just the opposite: human relationships and interactions are valued over arbitrary schedules and appointments. Many things may occur at once (since many people are involved in everything), and interruptions are frequent.

Situational Dialects

As the term implies, *situational dialects* are non-standard, specialized vocabularies associated with a wide variety of activities and situations. They perform various functions including:

1. speeding transactions such as boarding a bus, ordering a meal in a short-order restaurant, and buying theater tickets in New York;

2. enabling people in certain occupations and professions to communicate quickly and effectively with each other, for example, air traffic controllers, pilots, attorneys, physicians, mechanics, plumbers, electricians, etc.

Situational dialects are a kind of linguistic shorthand. When appropriate, learning them speeds acceptance into a subculture.

185

Reading List

Culture and Society

Hall, Edward T. *The Silent Language*. Garden City, NY: Anchor Press/ Doubleday, 1959.

———*The Hidden Dimension*. Garden City, NY: Anchor Press/ Doubleday, 1966.

———*Beyond Culture*. Garden City, NY: Anchor Press/Doubleday, 1976.

———*The Dance of Life: The Other Dimension of Time*. Garden City, NY: Anchor Press/Doubleday, 1983.

Lewis, Flora. *Europe: A Tapestry of Nations*. New York: Simon & Schuster, 1987.

The Germans

Anders, George. "Executive Style: Bosses in West Germany Stress Consensus Decision, Technical Know-How." *Wall Street Journal*, 25 September 1984.

Burmeister, Irmgard. *These Strange German Ways*. 14th ed. Hamburg: Atlantick-Brucke, 1980.

Clark, Lindley H. "Speaking of Business." *Wall Street Journal*, 7 June 1983.

Craig, Gordon. *The Germans.* New York: G.P. Putnam's Sons, 1982.

Drucker, Peter, F. "What We Can Learn from the Germans." *Wall Street Journal,* 6 March 1986.

Kramer, Jane. "Letter from West Germany." *New Yorker,* 19 December 1983.

Larson, Bob. *Getting Along with the Germans.* Esslingen am Neckar: Verlag Bechtle Esslingen, 1983.

Noelle-Neumann, Elisabeth. *The Germans: Public Opinion Polls, 1967-1980.* Westport, CT and London: Greenwood Press, 1981.

O'Boyle, Thomas F. "Success Stories: Three German Firms Show Heavy Industry Can Still Turn a Dollar." *Wall Street Journal,* 23 April 1986.

————"Sales Success: German Firms Stress Top Quality, Niches, to Keep Exports High." *Wall Street Journal,* 10 December 1987.

Solomon, Anthony M. "Germany Puts Savings over Jobs." *Wall Street Journal,* 24 March 1986.

Turner, Henry Ashby, Jr. *German Big Business and the Rise of Hitler.* New York: Oxford University Press, 1985.

U.S. Department of Commerce. "Foreign Economic Trends and Their Implications for the United States: Federal Republic of Germany." Semiannual publication available by subscription from Superintendent of Documents, GPO, Washington, DC 20402. Single copies may be obtained for a small fee from Publications Sales Branch, Rm. 1617, U.S. Department of Commerce, Washington, DC 20230.

The French

Ardagh, John. *France in the 1980s.* New York: Penguin Press, 1983.

Barzini, Luigi. *The Europeans.* New York: Simon & Schuster, 1983.

Beaudeux, Pierre. "Les Cadres Français? Des autocrates!" *L'Expansion,* September 1979.

Braudel, Fernand. *The Structure of Everyday Life.* New York: Harper & Row, 1982.

De Lacy, Justine. "The Sexy Computer." *Atlantic,* July 1987.

Elias, Norbert. *The Court Society.* New York: Pantheon, 1983.

Kramer, Jane. "Letter from Europe." *New Yorker,* 18 January 1982.

McCluggage, Denise. "I Remember It Distinctly." *Auto Week,* 26 November 1984.

Peyrefitte, Alain. *The Trouble with France.* New York: Knopf, 1981.

Reuzin, Philip. "French Visa Rule Gives More Americans Chance to Meet Champions at Bureaucracy." *Wall Street Journal,* 26 September 1986.

Suleiman, Ezra N. *Elites in French Society: The Politics of Survival.* Princeton, NJ: Princeton University Press, 1978.

U.S. Department of Commerce. "Foreign Economic Trends and Their Implications for the United States: France." Semi-annual publication available by subscription from Superintendent of Documents, GPO, Washington, DC 20402. Single copies may be obtained for a small fee from Publications Sales Branch, Room 1617, U.S. Department of Commerce, Washington, DC 20230.

Wylie, Laurence. *Village in the Vaucluse.* Cambridge, MA: Harvard University Press, 1972.

Zeldin, Theodore. *The French.* New York: Pantheon, 1983.

The Americans

Alden, Vernon R. "The Trade Deficit: Stop Looking For Scapegoats." *Business Week,* 8 April 1985.

Baldrige, Letitia. *Letitia Baldrige's Complete Guide to Executive Manners.* New York: Rawson Associates/Scribner's, 1985.

Barmash, Isadore. "European Retailers Find U.S. Difficult." *New York Times,* 15 January 1986.

Bloom, Allan. *The Closing of the American Mind.* New York: Simon & Schuster, Inc., 1987.

Boorstin, Daniel J. *The Americans: The Democratic Experience.* New York: Random House, 1973.

Brigham, Eugene F. *Financial Management: Theory and Practice.* 4th ed. Chicago: Dryden Press, 1977.

Deal, Terrence, and Allan Kennedy. *Corporate Cultures: The Rights and Rituals of Corporate Life.* Reading, MA: Addison-Wesley, 1982.

Drucker, Peter F. *Technology, Management and Society.* New York: Harper & Row, 1970.

———*The Concept of the Corporation.* New York: G.Y. Crowell, 1972.

———*Management Tasks, Responsibilities, Practices.* New York: Harper & Row, 1974.

———*Managing in Turbulent Times.* New York: Harper & Row, 1980.

———"Squeezing the Firm's Midriff Bulge." *Wall Street Journal,* 25 March 1983.

———"Playing in the Information-Based Orchestra." *Wall Street Journal,* 4 June 1985.

———*The Frontiers of Managment: Where Tomorrow's Decisions Are Being Shaped Today.* New York: Dutton, 1986.

———"How to Manage the Boss." *Wall Street Journal,* 1 August 1986.

Eurich, Nell. *Corporate Classrooms.* Princeton, NJ: Princeton University Press, 1985.

Fong, Diana. "Learning to Do It Their Way." *Forbes,* 15 December 1986.

Garfield, Charles. *Peak Performers: The New Heroes of American Business.* New York: William Morrow, 1986.

Garreau, Joel. *The Nine Nations of North America.* Boston: Houghton-Mifflin, 1981.

Halberstam, David. *The Reckoning.* New York: William Morrow, 1986.

Hall, Edward T., and Mildred Reed Hall. *Hidden Differences: Doing Business with the Japanese.* Garden City, NY: Doubleday, 1987.

Harrington, Diana, and Brent D. Wilson. *Corporate Financial Analysis.* Plano, TX: Business Publications, Inc., 1983.

Hayes, Robert H. "Why Strategy Planning Goes Awry." *New York Times,* 20 April 1986.

Hennig, Margaret, and Anne Jardim. *The Managerial Woman.* Garden City, NY: Anchor Press/Doubleday, 1977.

Hirsch, E.D., Jr. *Cultural Literacy.* Boston: Houghton Mifflin Company, 1987.

Hymowitz, Carol, and Timothy D. Schellhardt, eds. "The Glass Ceiling." *Wall Street Journal.* Special Report on the Corporate Woman, 24 March 1986.

Iacocca, Lee. *Iacocca, An Autobiography.* New York: Bantam Books, 1984.

Jacobs, Nehama, and Sarah Hardesty. *Success and Betrayal: The Crisis of Women in Corporate America.* New York: Franklin Watts, 1986.

Larson, Erik. "Why Are Some Managers Top Performers?" *Wall Street Journal,* 21 January 1983.

Lasch, Christopher. *The Culture of Narcissism: American Life in an Age of Diminishing Expectations.* New York: Warner Books, 1979.

Lazer, William. *Handbook of Demographics for Marketing and Advertising: Sources and Trends on the American Consumer.* Lexington, MA: Lexington Books, 1987.

Lazer, William, and James Culley. *Marketing Management: Fundamentals and Practices.* Boston: Houghton Mifflin, 1982.

McCall, Morgan W., Jr., and Michael M. Lombardo. "What Makes a Top Executive?" *Psychology Today,* February 1983.

Miller, Arthur. *Death of a Salesman.* New York: Viking Press, 1949.

Mills, C. Wright. *The Power Elite.* New York: Oxford University Press, 1956.

Nadler, Paul S. *Commercial Banking in the Economy.* 3rd ed. New York: Random House, 1979.

Peters, Thomas J., and Robert H. Waterman, Jr. *In Search of Excellence: Lessons from American's Best-Run Companies.* New York: Harper & Row, 1982.

Ringer, Robert J. *Looking Out for Number One.* New York: Fawcett Books, 1978.

Sabel, Charles F., and Gary B. Herrigel. "Losing a Market to a High-Wage Nation." *New York Times,* 14 June 1987.

Sharfman, William L. "Corporate Images vs. Corporate Mission." *Marketing Review,* January/February 1981.

Sloan, Alfred. *My Years with General Motors.* Garden City, NY: Doubleday, 1972.

Time. "Immigrants: The Changing Face of America." Special Issue. 8 July 1985.
"Minding Our Manners Again." 8 November 1984.

Tocqueville, Alexis de. *Democracy in America.* 1835-1840. (Numerous editions.)

Whyte, William H., Jr. *The Organization Man.* New York: Touchstone Books, 1972.

Wysocki, Bernard. "Culture Clash: Doing Business in Different Lands." *Wall Street Journal,* 20 May 1985.

Index

193